ADLAI E. STEVENSON
OF ILLINOIS

BY NOEL F. BUSCH

Designed by GEORGE HORNBY

GOVERNOR ADLAI E. STEVENSON

Adlai E.
STEVENSON
of Illinois

A PORTRAIT BY

Noel F. Busch

Farrar, Straus & Young : *New York*

Designed by GEORGE HORNBY

Foreword

The author wishes to make it unmistakably clear that this book is in no sense an "authorized" biography; and that it is not to be construed by any stretch of the imagination as any sort of political gesture on the part of the subject.

1

Aᴅʟᴀɪ (almost rhymes with "gladly") Eᴡɪɴɢ Sᴛᴇᴠᴇɴꜱᴏɴ, thirty-second governor of the state of Illinois and one of the few men in history who has turned down a sure nomination for the presidency of the United States before being elected to that office, is an earnest, urbane, and affable man of fifty-two who weighs one hundred and eighty-five pounds, stands five feet nine and a half inches, speaks with an Eastern accent, has an income of some $50,000 a year including his salary of $12,000, owns a Dalmatian dog called Artie, wears Brooks Brothers shirts, hates to leave an electric light burning in an empty room and has a detached viewpoint about his sudden emergence as a major figure on the world scene which sometimes pleases, sometimes pains and always puzzles professional politicians who are accustomed to a very different attitude on the part of such political luminaries.

Stevenson's self-possession under trying circumstances is not a newly acquired characteristic. In 1937, when he was practicing law in Chicago as a partner in the firm of Cutting, Moore and Sidley, Stevenson and his wife, the former Ellen Borden, from whom he was divorced in 1949, decided to build a house in the country. They acquired seventy acres of choice real estate in Libertyville, near the fashionable suburb of Lake Forest, where they had previously spent their summers. There they invested some thirty thousand dollars in a small but elegant dwelling in the modern style, with steel walls and picture windows. Six weeks after they had moved themselves and their belongings into it, the house caught fire on an evening when they were not at home. A dispute arose among local fire companies as to which one was responsible for the area in which the property was located. When several engines finally arrived, there was further controversy as to which one should do what. Finally, the water supply proved unsatisfactory for the purposes at hand. By the time the Stevensons reached the scene of the conflagration, it was too late for anyone to do much, except stand around and watch the structure burn to the ground.

One of the neighbors who was near Stevenson in the crowd of spectators edged over to express his sympathy. As he did so a bit of burning debris floated through the air and dropped at the owner's feet. Stevenson picked it up and calmly lit a cigarette with it.

"Oh, well," he said, "as you can see, we are still using the house."

Stevenson's ability to achieve minor *mots* in moments of stress is less the result of flippancy on his part than of an overly strict conscience, which operates in a peculiar fashion. To begin with, Stevenson's conscience obliges him to set himself unusually high standards of efficiency and deportment. Then it forbids him to seek the sympathy of outsiders in what he regards as his own inexcusable failure to live up to these standards. Thus, on the occasion of the conflagration, Stevenson was not only shocked and saddened by the ruin of a project into which he and his wife had poured much money, thought and effort. He was also mortified by the realization that, while the structure itself was insured, the newly assembled contents, including many items of family memorabilia by which he set great store, were both unprotected and irreplaceable. To have betrayed his inward feelings, however, would have seemed to Stevenson unpardonable and might have caused him more remorse than the loss of his property.

Many people take a somewhat similarly Spartan attitude toward life but Stevenson goes much further than the stoic norm. Part of his Spartan attitude is to seem not to take one and to appear, insofar as possible, in the role of a carefree, casual hedonist. Stevenson owes much of his success first in private and later in public life to a remarkable proficiency in the role of trouble-shooter, as successively, a corporation lawyer, a Washington bureaucrat, a diplomat, and a state executive. However, in addition to commanding him to work hard and effectively, his conscience forbids him to take apparent pride in the results of doing so. In order to avoid what might seem to him an undue claim upon public approbation, Stevenson has formed the habit of telling stories on himself which show him in the light of a comedy character, who never does anything right and can be counted on to make a hash of anything he undertakes. Long practice at this form of deception has made Stevenson so adept at it that he sometimes almost succeeds in fooling himself.

Just before flying to the March 31st Jefferson-Jackson Day dinner in Washington, at which Truman announced his long-deferred decision not to run again, Stevenson was discussing with an old friend and close political associate his promise to appear, the day after the dinner, on the television program, *Meet the Press*.

"Now, why do I get myself into these things?" Stevenson demanded angrily. "I ought to know better. Damn it, I simply can't understand how I can be such a fool. Anyway, it was a mistake. I'll wire to say I've thought it over and just don't feel that I can do it."

Stevenson's associate counseled against this course, on the ground that it would greatly inconvenience the producer and everyone else on the program.

"Oh, well, I suppose I've got to go through with it," said the Governor. "I won't know what to say, though. They'll ask me a lot of hard questions and I won't know any of the answers. I'll plumber the whole thing, as usual."

As to the questions he would be asked, Stevenson's worst forebodings were amply justified. The President's unforeseen announcement had made Stevenson overnight the most talked-about man in the country and the reporters were naturally eager to make the most of their opportunity. Stevenson, however, acquitted himself admirably and gave such satisfactory answers that his own stature as a possible candidate was substantially increased. On his return to Springfield, he was, as usual, dissatisfied with his performance.

"I don't think I did a good job at all," he remarked firmly, "and anyway, now look what I've got myself into!"

Stevenson's habitual air of aggrieved if not downright indignant self-deprecation would be disarming in almost anyone, but in a man who has been widely regarded as well-qualified for the biggest job in the nation, if not the world, it seems to the casual observer especially refreshing. Political experts however take a different view about such matters. Potential presidential candidates are supposed to be over-stuffed with assurance, on the perhaps specious premise that obvious self-confidence is the first prerequisite for enlisting the confidence of their fellow citizens. Thus, any potential candidate who, like Stevenson, openly shows self-doubt, is put down as a subtle schemer artfully acting the role in a new way. Stevenson's skeptical attitude toward his own quali-fications, along with his outspoken reluctance to quit his present job as governor, were thus speedily diagnosed by the deep thinkers as complementary parts of a shrewdly devised political strategy.

Stevenson himself is more entertained than aggrieved by such interpretations. "I must confess," he remarked recently, "I seem to spend a lot of time reading about myself in papers and magazines these days. The awful thing is, I can't say that I mind it much either." The Governor's official car, a monumental Cadillac limousine, is a dozen years old and has gone more than three hundred thousand miles. This vehicle, and a pair of ten-year-old golf shoes with the spikes removed which he habitually wears around Springfield, have become symbols of his personal parsimoniousness and Stevenson, in a good-humored way, likes to admit that he is fully aware of the political effect of such homespun affections. The Governor, in point of fact, has excellent taste in clothes and wears them quite well enough to get on a list of the ten thousand best-dressed Americans, if there were such a thing. That he already had plenty of suits is probably the main reason why, as is frequently pointed out, he has bought none since he arrived in Springfield, except a gray flannel one which his sister persuaded him to have run up by a local tailor.

The Governor's sister, Mrs. Ernest L. Ives, who might well become at least a part-time first lady in case Stevenson ever took up residence in the White House, is a vivacious brunette, whose social background might make her, too, unusually well-qualified for such a locale. Two and a half years older than the Governor, she made her debut in Washington in 1918, when their father was serving as special assistant to the then Secretary of the Navy, Josephus Daniels, whose literary son, Jonathan, is now one of Stevenson's close friends. Subsequently, she got interested in acting and appeared professionally opposite Sidney Blackmer in the Detroit, New York and Boston run of a Rafael Sabatini play in 1925. Her marriage to Ernest Ives, a member of a propertied Virginia family, who was then a career foreign service officer, took place in Italy the next year, and her presentation at the Court of St. James in 1931. The Iveses, who have a grown son, Timothy, now in the air force, spent the next ten years or so *en poste* in Europe or Africa. Nowadays, when not in Springfield, they spend most of their time at Southern Pines, N. C., where they have a farm, or at the old Stevenson family house on Washington Street in Bloomington, sixty miles north of Springfield on the Gulf, Mobile and Ohio line. When the Iveses are not in Springfield, the Governor and William McCormick Blair Jr., one of his administrative assistants, are the only full-time occupants of the Executive Mansion which, however, is usually quite densely populated by an ample non-resident staff and by a constant stream of visitors, official and otherwise.

Built in 1856, in the solidly ornate style of its era, the mansion is a three-story white brick and stone edifice which stands on a slight eminence just south of the main business district of the capital, a busy town of some 80,000 souls. It is surrounded by an acre or so of rather sparsely planted lawn, of which the two most conspicuous features are a walled garden and barbecue pit at the rear and a three-story bird-mansion in the same style, though somewhat smaller, than the human one. Callers at the latter arrive by an uphill concrete driveway that divides just before the front door, one branch leading to the front steps and the other branch going under the steps to a door that opens into the basement where the Governor and several members of his personal staff have offices.

Under the steps and across the subway-drive from the basement door of the mansion is a cubbyhole usually occupied by one of four state policemen who take turns guarding the house, admitting callers, and acting as drivers of the Cadillac or a smaller car which the Governor also often drives himself. The head of the police detail is a ruddy, cheerful man named Captain William Van Diver, whose wife has been the mansion housekeeper for the past dozen years. The indoor domestic staff, all colored, includes Gilbert Wright and Robert Jones, the butler and second man, and Mrs. Gertrude Dent, the cook, as well as two maids and a stair-and-woodwork polisher. The Van Divers live in an apartment over the converted coachhouse garage, and all the servants live out.

The Governor and Blair occupy rooms on the third floor of the mansion, where six high-ceilinged bedrooms surround a central stair well.

The Governor's bedroom, with white plaster walls and green-carpeted floor, is furnished, like the rest of the mansion, in a haphazard style partly indicative of Stevenson's taste but mostly of that of previous occupants. The pictures on the walls include small portrait engravings of Mr. and Mrs. Jesse W. Fell, the Governor's favorites among his numerous noteworthy ancestors, and a big, vaguely impressionistic painting of a Mexican boy holding a white rooster. Over the bed hangs the coat-of-arms of the Willis family, one of several patrician clans included in the Governor's long list of colonial forbears, with the motto *"Comiter et Fortiter."* The books on the bedside table recently included *The Bible as an Inspiration, The Book of Proverbs, Overweight and Underweight,* and *Dr. Johnson's Prayer Book.*

The Governor, a stickler for punctuality who often carries two Elgin watches, one on his wrist and one on a waistcoat chain to balance a key-ring at the other end, arises at seven-thirty every morning and breakfasts at eight-thirty sharp, on bacon and eggs, codfish balls, or some other substantial dish. Whether or not guests are present, breakfast conversation is sparse. The Governor eats with one hand only, using the other hand and both eyes to run through the Chicago *Tribune* and *Sun-Times,* and Springfield's *Illinois State Journal.* At nine or a minute or two thereafter, he pushes his chair back and goes downstairs to work.

The walls of the Governor's office are hung, and its furnishings embellished, with family portraits, photographs and mementoes. The largest of these is an old print showing the winner of an election bet on his grandfather, Adlai Ewing Stevenson the first, who served as Vice-President from 1892 to 1896, being pulled through the streets of Chicago in a carriage by the loser. Stevenson's desk, under two windows at the end of the room, fronts a long conference table of which one end is contiguous with it in T-formation. A door on the Governor's right leads into a smaller room where his two secretaries, Miss Carol Evans and Mrs. Margaret Munn, have their desks. Artie, the Dalmatian, usually lies under the latter desk, with his tail sticking out in a fashion that sometimes alarms shortsighted visitors who mistake it for some sort of speckled snake.

Artie, a rather sooty-looking specimen of his breed, whose real name is King Arthur, has a gloomy temperament which may be partly the result of upbringing and environment. First he was left alone early in life owing to the death of his father, Merlin, and the removal to others parts of his brother, Sir Launcelot. Then, when his master's home broke up, he was brought from the farm at Libertyville, where he could go and come as he pleased, to the mansion whose main attraction, from the Dalmatian point of view, was perhaps the post that supported the bird house. Even the fascinations of this fixture did not prove inexhaustible. Artie presently took to running around the neighborhood at night, in disregard of a city ordinance that prohibits such canine behavior. This resulted in phone calls from the neighbors, who frequently reported his misdeeds to the mansion police detail.

"Artie is a constant source of embarrassment to the state

police and to me too," say the Governor. "After all, a Governor's dog may not have to be above suspicion but he should at least try to obey the law. Still, I'm afraid Artie really has a miserable life here, so we try to make allowances."

Across the hall from the secretaries' office is a similar one occupied by Blair, a product of Groton, Stanford, and the China-Burma-India theater of World War II, who joined the Governor's staff two years ago. Blair is a slightly renegade member of a well-known Chicago family which includes the redoubtable Colonel Robert McCormick, who is his father's first cousin. His role in the Governor's entourage involves screening visitors, handling appointments, and dealing with social as well as official invitations. Adjacent to his office and across the hall from the Governor's is another larger office in which sit another secretary, Mrs. Francis Ruys, and the Governor's top administrative assistant, Carl McGowan. McGowan, five years older than Blair and at forty the senior member of Stevenson's personal staff, worked with the Governor in Washington during the war and two years ago quit a law professorship at Northwestern to rejoin his staff. His responsibilities, somewhat analogous to those usually handled by the legal vice-president in a major business organization, including mapping legislative strategy when the General Assembly is in session, helping to plan and draft legislation when it isn't and advising the Governor on most of his important legal and administrative problems and policies.

Stevenson himself usually works straight through the day, sometimes lunching from a tray at his desk but more often going upstairs to the smaller of the two dining rooms with Blair, McGowan or whatever visitors are present. About six-thirty in the afternoon he quits his desk in time for a rather hasty "bourbon toddy" before dinner, which takes place at seven or very soon thereafter. "Bourbon toddy" is whiskey and water with ice and a little sugar.

During his years in private legal practice the Governor fell into the habit of doing a good deal of work at night, when he and his wife were not entertaining or dining with friends. Mrs. Stevenson now lives either in her Chicago apartment or in weekend quarters near the house at Liberty-ville which the Governor still owns and now rents to his friend, Marshall Field Jr., the publisher of the *Sun-Times.* The Stevensons' two older boys, Adlai III and Borden, are at Harvard, in their senior and freshman years respectively. Their fifteen-year-old brother, John Fell, is at nearby Milton Academy. When the boys come back for holidays, they spend half their time with their mother. With family and social obligations thus reduced to a minimum, Stevenson, despite the urgings of his aides that he should relax more, is more than ever inclined to put in long evenings as well as full days at his desk. The Governor used to ride a good deal, play golf in the nineties and tennis a little better. Nowadays, except for a little weekend tennis and an occasional early morning or late evening walk, he takes no exercise whatever, so far without discernible ill effects upon either his health or spirits.

Much of Stevenson's work, now and in the past, has consisted of reading over documents, either previously dictated by himself or addressed to him by others. When so engaged, he often rests his forehead on his right finger tips, a habit which has resulted in a fine, diagonal crease inter-

ADLAI E. STEVENSON

secting four other shallow wrinkles that cross his brow horizontally. The Governor has a high, slightly freckled forehead, on which the hair line has been in slow retreat for some years; bright blue eyes, for which he wears horn-rimmed glasses when reading; a mobile, sensitive mouth and a slightly aquiline nose which is off center to the left as the result of three fractures during an exceptionally embattled boyhood. He usually carries his head slightly forward, listens intently when someone is talking to him and speaks in a low-keyed but resonant voice, choosing his words adroitly and using a considerable range of tempo and modulation to accentuate shades of meaning.

While not by any means an English or even a Rooseveltian New York accent — the Governor often says "acrosst" for "across" and indulges in several other regional eccentricities — Stevenson's speech, influenced by family precept, travel in Europe and an Eastern schooling, is so different from the variety normally heard in his native habitat that it often causes comment, not always of a favorable nature. Indeed, his accent nearly blighted his political career at the outset, when Colonel Jacob M. Arvey, the astute Chicago political boss who is usually credited with having been the first to recognize Stevenson's political possibilities in 1947, was informed by suspicious colleagues that Stevenson had gone to Oxford. Aware that no Oxford product could hope to get anywhere politically in a town whose Mayor Big Bill Thompson used to get elected regularly on a platform promise, never kept, to "bust King George in the snoot" and whose foremost newspaper proprietor, himself schooled in England, is forever snubbing the British for snobbism,

Arvey was horrified by this news. Meeting a friend of Stevenson's on a train, he whispered the scandal in his ear and asked if there was any way that the ugly rumor could be run to earth. The friend wired Stevenson and got a reassuring denial: "Never went to Oxford not even to Eton." This put Stevenson's political career back on the tracks.

Stevenson has been described as, among other things, "a Prairie Roosevelt," a "Chicago Galahad" and an "Abe Lincoln in a buttoned-down shirt." While none of these epithets are altogether accurate, all are at least suggestive of the unmistakable incongruity between the Governor and the run of U. S. politicians generally and of Mid-West politicians in particular. Even if Stevenson's emergence from the shadows of state politics to the brightly lighted center of the national stage had taken place gradually, and even if it had been preceded by the fanfare that usually announces the entrance of freshmen aspirants to high office who turn up in any presidential year, the mass of voters might still have a fairly hard time getting used to, and understanding such an unusual sort of performer in such a role. However, instead of getting on stage on cue and gradually, Stevenson burst on with a suddenness which would have been disconcerting even in the case of the customary hard-breathing rostrum-athletes prepared to wear funny hats, give one-man talk-athons, or turn ideological cart-wheels in the effort to attract votes. The consequence of all this has been, not unnaturally, some confusion on the part of the voting public as to just what Stevenson stands for, where he came from and even who he is, as well as just how it developed all of a sudden, one week in January of 1952, that the answers to these questions assumed profound national significance.

2

WHETHER OR NOT Stevenson runs for President in 1952, or, for that matter, ever, his emergence from the comparative obscurity of state government in Springfield to the position of front-runner and sure winner in the Democratic party sweepstakes in the space of less than three months is without precedent in the far from short and simple annals of the U. S. presidency. At the conclusion of this dazzling sprint — of which by no means the least remarkable feature was that it ended long before the wire, when the Governor obligingly jogged off the track to watch his less fleet competitors fight each other down the homestretch — Stevenson was so far ahead that the rest of the field was out of sight behind him. The start, however, was a very different matter. This took place largely by accident one evening in late August of 1951, when a young man named Porter McKeever, then press chief for the U. S. mission to the United Nations to whose General Assembly Stevenson had been an alternate delegate in 1946 and 1947, dined with Frank Montero, secretary of an organization called the National Urban League, in New York.

During the course of casual conversation, Montero mentioned that the League, of which one function is to stimulate public discussion of racial relations, was making plans for its annual dinner the next January. The banquet committee, it seemed, had invited Stevenson as a main speaker and was wondering what to ask him to talk about. McKeever casually suggested that a possible theme for his speech might be the effect of racial discrimination in the U. S. upon U. S. relations with, and propaganda in, foreign countries, especially those in Asia. He remarked that Stevenson qualified as an expert on that topic, both as an outstanding supporter of civil rights at home and as a public servant of wide experience abroad.

McKeever left for Europe a few days later but his suggestion stuck in Montero's mind. Other active members of the League thought well of it. Stevenson, who had made a habit of giving three or four speeches outside his state every year, thought both the occasion and the subject sounded worth-while. He accepted the invitation and then went on with his job which, shortly afterwards, came to include an investigation into a tragic mine disaster at West Frankfort, Illinois, where over a hundred miners were killed by an explosion.

At about the same time that the Urban League was making plans for its banquet, a totally unrelated conference about other plans was going on in the editorial offices of *Time,* whose editor, T. S. Matthews, had been a 1922 classmate and close friend of Stevenson at Princeton. *Time's* Chicago bureau had proposed Stevenson as a subject for a "cover story" and his qualifications, based on his record as Governor, were being carefully canvassed. Eventually, the conclusion was reached that they were adequate. The question that then arose was when the cover should be scheduled. January looked like a good month, for one reason and another. In November, a query went to Chicago: "Is Stevenson doing anything that might possibly make news that month?" The Chicago bureau consulted Blair in the Governor's office, who mentioned that the Governor would be going to New York to deliver his Urban League speech on the twenty-first. *Time* decided that, although the story was intended to be chiefly a "take-out on the always fascinating state of Illinois," the New York speech would make an adequate "news-peg."

At about the same time that these two distantly related series of events were taking place, a third sequence was starting in Washington, in the form of certain thoughts that passed through the mind of President Harry S. Truman. Early in January, these thoughts caused Mr. Truman to send word to Governor Stevenson that he hoped, the next time the Governor was in Washington, that he would come to pay a call.

The link between Truman's suggestion, the *Time* cover story and the Urban League dinner proved to be the catastrophe at West Frankfort. This, and the ensuing investigation into its causes, gave sudden impetus to legislation then before Congress to place mine investigation under federal rather than state authority. Stevenson, a confirmed believer in the theory that government should be as decentralized as possible, opposed the idea and wanted to make his views known to John L. Lewis, Oscar Chapman and other influential proponents of the law in question. Thus, instead of being a cause of postponing his trip East, as might otherwise have been the case, the disaster was an additional cause for making it.

The Governor flew to New York on Sunday, the twentieth of January. His speech at the Urban League dinner, held in the grand ballroom of the Waldorf, went off well on Monday night, and inspired a laudatory editorial in the New York *Herald Tribune* the next day. The Governor had planned to fly to Washington on Tuesday, the twenty-second, but the morning turned out to be a miserably rainy one. Most planes were grounded — though not the one on which former Secretary of War Robert Patterson was a passenger and which crashed at Newark, killing everyone on board. The Governor and Blair, who had gone East with him, caught a noon train for Washington and arrived about four o'clock. When they reached the Metropolitan Club, where they had planned to stay, it developed that the club had no rooms but had made reservations for them at the Roger-Smith Hotel. Blair and the Governor proceeded thither, taking with them a sheaf of telephone messages that had been waiting them. One of the messages was from the White House and led to the arrangement by which, after dining rather hurriedly with a former office associate named George Ball, the Governor entered the front door of Blair House at eight-thirty that evening. Stevenson returned to his hotel around eleven and, the next morning, breakfasted with Illinois' junior Senator, Paul Douglas.

When a presidential caller stays for two hours of private chat with the chief executive, Washington reporters naturally become curious. Under the circumstances existing at that moment, which were that Truman had already hinted that he might not run again, their curiosity about Stevenson's call was more intense than it would have been otherwise. By the following afternoon, Stevenson's name was, accordingly, spread from coast to coast in the headlines, and while no one except Truman and the Governor knew then exactly what had been said, it was not hard to draw a reasonable inference. By Wednesday evening the Governor had been photographed dozens of times by all the leading news agencies, and the political columnists had begun to speculate seriously about his future. It was not until the next day, however, that *Time* came out with his picture on the cover.

In researching the cover story, *Time's* diligent Chicago correspondent, William Glasgow, had sent in some thirty pages of exhaustive information on the Governor. Other correspondents had sent in as much again from other sources all over the U. S. In the course of preparing the story itself, *Time* had naturally got wind of the visit to Blair House well before it happened; and it was this, rather than the Urban League dinner, that became the "news-peg" for an exhaustive biographical sketch. The net effect was to convince readers unaware of the intricacies of the publishing business that the editors of the nation's major news magazine considered Stevenson's call on the President the major event of the week — which indeed, partly on that very account, it speedily became.

By the time Stevenson boarded a Thursday morning plane for Chicago — on which a fellow passenger, by pure coincidence, proved to be his old United Nations colleague, John Foster Dulles, thus giving rise to further speculation when they landed together — Stevenson had become a major presidential possibility. Thereafter, the Stevenson boom gained momentum with rapidity possibly unmatched since

William Jennings Bryan took the nation by storm with his Cross of Gold speech in 1896.

If the start of Stevenson's presidential boom was sensational, what followed was even more so. This began with an appraisal by political experts of precisely what the excitement was all about. The astonishing thing about Stevenson, it developed, was not that President Truman and the rest of the nation had discovered him simultaneously in January 1952 but that both had not discovered him long before. The coincidence whereby several forces pushing Stevenson toward the White House had suddenly combined to give him a jet-propelled takeoff might indeed have been an accident. The forces themselves were not only logical but apparently so irresistible as to defy consistent metaphor.

On starting to investigate the validity of the Stevenson claim, the first thing the experts did was naturally to scratch around on the surface in search of biographical data. This promptly revealed a deep vein of pure gold. It developed that Stevenson came from a family which, in the state of Illinois, politically more strategic than New York, amounted to an equivalent of the Roosevelt family in their less clan-conscious state, save that it included no captains in the China trade or other dubious characters.

Having examined Stevenson's personal credentials, the experts next proceeded to examine his political ones. These proved to be, if possible, even more impressive. In 1948, when Truman barely carried Illinois by 34,000 votes, Stevenson had been elected governor by a landslide majority of 572,000, largest in Illinois history. This vote might have been to some degree attributable to the squalid character of his predecessor's administration, but Stevenson was, it seemed, more than a mere vote getter. In his subsequent three years in office, in a state long characterized by incorrigible crookery, he had built up a record which was causing Illinois to compare him with John Peter Altgeld, celebrated as "The Eagle Forgotten" by Illinois' late poet laureate, Vachel Lindsay, who lived across the street from the Executive Mansion.

As to the cause of the President's apparent enthusiasm for Stevenson, that appeared to rest upon an even stronger basis than had at first glance been apparent. Since Stevenson had far outrun the President in Illinois, he was probably entitled to most of the credit for keeping that important state in the Democratic column. However, what was perhaps even more consequential than the debt of gratitude which Truman obviously owed Stevenson, was the fact that the Governor had never made the slightest effort to collect it. Ordinarily, a governor who merely rides to success on a presidential bandwagon is likely to feel that he deserves some sort of reward if only for not falling off. In this case, as the politicoes were quick to observe, the President had been, in effect, a hitch-hiker on the Stevenson bandwagon; but instead of commuting to Washington to seek the prizes to which he was so clearly entitled, Stevenson had stayed in Illinois and attended to state business. Far from asking favors of Truman, he had conferred another one on him in the form of an unusually eloquent welcoming speech when the President visited Chicago for the Jefferson Jubilee in May, 1950.

Stevenson himself, when the jostling experts got close enough to peek over each others' shoulders for a close look, proved to be an eminently personable and pleasant dignitary, whose qualifications for the White House improved upon acquaintance. The Governor, it developed, was not merely a good after-dinner speaker but easily the best all-around political orator to appear on the U. S. scene since F.D.R. His radio voice was only surpassed by his presence on television. Finally, wonder of wonders, he was the first major U. S. public figure in a generation who in addition to delivering a speech could even write one, a capacity long since found only in English-speaking politicians on the opposite side of the Atlantic.

Stevenson wrote more than speeches. He could even turn out smooth professional pieces for top U. S. publications like *Foreign Affairs* and the *Atlantic Monthly* and had just proved it with the lead article in each. The subjects of these essays were U. S. foreign policy, especially in regard to Korea, and U. S. morals, especially in regard to political corruption and crime, which were sure to be, respectively, the major U. S. foreign and domestic issues in the campaign of 1952. Stevenson qualified not as a theorist but as a practical authority on both, since smashing gambling and corruption was one of his top gubernatorial feats in Illinois and since foreign policy had been his chief metier for most of his adult life prior to his election.

There was only one thing left for the goggle-eyed experts to do after adding all this up. That was to compare Stevenson with the rest of the field in the Democratic party. When they did so, the results were startling. The party had, to be sure, a half dozen or so fairly sound bits of presidential timber lying around, such as Vinson, Harriman, Kefauver, Kerr,

Lausche, and Russell. What with one thing or another however, it turned out that all the boards had knots in them, in the form of faulty geography, old age, inability to articulate, dis-sympathy with the President or whatever. In short, it became clear not only that Stevenson was a candidate of heroic stature but also that there was no one else whose qualifications were even faintly comparable.

The only possible objection that could be made to Stevenson after a careful appraisal of the situation seemed to be that he was still, despite the furore about the Blair House meeting, relatively unknown outside his own state. This weakness was speedily remedied by a spate of articles, picture stories, evaluations and interviews in newspapers, magazines and on the major radio and television networks. Political pundits like Marquis Childs, Joseph Alsop and Ernest Lindley convened at the Executive Mansion; the Governor's personal mail, which had previously averaged a hundred or so letters a week jumped to three hundred a day; his office staff was deluged by telegrams and phone calls. Meanwhile, the one point which, if it had not been exactly overlooked in the excitement, had never been decided was the Governor's own reaction to it all.

By the middle of April rough estimates of the situation showed that Stevenson could certainly win the nomination with ease if not on the first ballot then, at latest, on the second. It was at this juncture that Stevenson, theretofore in the position of a man who has won the grand prize in a sweepstakes without even buying a ticket, cleared up the uncertainty, at least temporarily, by announcing that he could not run.

Stevenson's announcement read in full as follows:

"I have been urged to announce my candidacy for the Democratic nomination for President, but I am a candidate for Governor of Illinois and I cannot run for two offices at the same time. Moreover, my duties as Governor do not presently afford the time to campaign for the nomination even if I wanted it.

"Others have asked me merely to say that I would accept a nomination which I did not seek. To state my position now on a prospect so remote in time and probability seems to me a little presumptuous. But I would rather presume than embarrass or mislead.

"In these somber years the hopes of mankind dwell with the President of the United States. From such dread responsibility one does not shrink in fear, self-interest or humility. But great political parties, like great nations, have no indispensable man, and last January, before I was even considered for the presidency, I announced that I would seek re-election as Governor of Illinois. Last week I was nominated in the Democratic primary. It is the highest office within the gift of the citizens of Illinois, and its power for good or ill over their lives is correspondingly great. No one should lightly aspire to it or lightly abandon the quest once begun.

"Hence, I have repeatedly said that I was a candidate for Governor of Illinois and had no other ambition. To this I must now add that in view of my prior commitment to run for governor and my desire and the desire of many who have given me their help and confidence in our unfinished work in Illinois, I could not accept the nomination for any other office this summer.

"Better state government is the only sound foundation for our federal system, and I am proud and content to stand on my commitment to ask the people of Illinois to allow me to continue for another four years in my present post.

"I cannot hope that my situation will be universally understood or my conclusions unanimously approved.

"I can hope that friends with larger ambitions for me will not think ill of me. They have paid me the greatest compliment within their gift, and they have my utmost gratitude."

Many incumbent presidents, from Washington to Truman, have refused to succeed themselves. A few military figures have indicated their unwillingness to enter a new branch of public service — like Eisenhower, who, however, reconsidered four years later, or General Sherman, whose famous statement actually preceded anything in the nature of a serious boom. A good many politicians who might conceivably have won a nomination by campaigning for it have thought better of doing so, like Senator Vandenberg in 1944. What made Stevenson's statement unique was that he was not in any one of these categories; and no practicing politician, actually assured of a presidential nomination, has ever before declined one.

A few days after making his statement, the Governor was asked whether, without altering or amplifying it in any way, he would give a sort of play-by-play account of how he had reached his decision. Stevenson said:

"Well, I suppose I had to start thinking about it after visiting with the President and all the ensuing speculation. I began to receive visitations from groups, mostly of two sorts. One was composed mostly of Democratic politicoes. The other was mostly of newspaper people — largely Eisenhower supporters who were apprehensive that he would not be named and that our foreign policy might be endangered by Taft. So I found myself beset by these two kinds of groups — the pro-Eisenhower people and the politicoes.

"The long agony that followed was never about what I wanted to do — I had already settled that. It was the result of an increasing pressure to get me to do something different.

"As far as I was concerned, I had the conviction that having made my bed, I should lie in it. Having announced that I was going to run for governor, I shouldn't be diverted from doing it by any deliberate or voluntary act on my part. We had started a lot of things here that I wanted to finish. I dreaded, for instance, to see what might happen to our highway program. I didn't want to see our welfare program slip back into the old muddy routine. Then there were many other things. As I said in that statement, I felt an obligation to a lot of people who had come down here to help me, and a lot of citizens who had given me their confidence and support. However, I began to see for a certainty that if I just made a statement to the effect that I wouldn't *campaign* for the nomination, people were going to make a candidate out of me anyway. Then I would find myself in the very distasteful position of running for two offices at the same time. I should add that I have no ambition to be President. That nobody will believe, but it's the truth.

"So it all added up to the inescapable conclusion that I would have to make a statement — or else be in the position of letting down a lot of other friends who wanted me to run, not to mention the political leaders who wanted to make their own commitments. Sometimes, you know they like to take an early position so that they can refer to it when convenient later on.

"There really wasn't any time when I was close to giving an affirmative answer, the only question was whether I had to give any answer. The things that gave me pause were first the gross presumption of turning down something that hadn't been offered to me — that was just a matter of taste, and I didn't like to do it. Then there was the matter of the office of the presidency; I didn't like to seem to be putting the presidency below the governorship of a state. And then I didn't want to seem to be expressing a fear of the office. I don't think I'm a very humble man in any Christian sense of the word but at the same time I just didn't feel that I had any God-given powers to figure out the solution to coexistence with the Soviet Union and all our other tremendous problems. I had no such self-confidence at all but yet I didn't want to seem to shrink from the job out of fear. I didn't want it — it seemed to me to mean honor, yes, but also misery. Nor could I overlook the implications of pitiless publicity for my children. But at the same time I wasn't going to shrink from it or wave it away with any maudlin nonsense about 'I'm not man enough, the burdens are too dreadful, and I can't do it.'

"I had hoped at first that just by taking a negative attitude, the situation might take care of itself. But as it began to get increasingly clear that that wasn't going to work, I had to think about another way. Then the question began to be how, when and where to say it.

"Oh, I suppose I considered saying 'yes,' of course. There was the view that a nomination for the presidency is just

Maternal grandparents of Governor Adlai E. Stevenson. W. O. Davis was a clerk for Jesse W. Fell, his wife's father, and later founded the Bloomington *Pantagraph*.

Adlai E. Stevenson I and Adlai E. Stevenson II in July, 1900, when the former was running for the vice-presidency on the ticket headed by William Jennings Bryan.

Letitia Green Stevenson, the Governor's paternal grandmother. One of the most indefatigable clubwomen in U. S. history, Mrs. Stevenson helped found the D.A.R.

Jesse W. Fell, the Governor's great-grandfather, was a tailor, lawyer, editor, teacher, industrialist and Quaker politico who was responsible for the Lincoln-Douglas debates.

Children of Adlai E. Stevenson I: left to right, Letitia, Julia, Lewis and Mary. Lewis Stevenson, the Governor's father, went to school at Exeter.

Four generations of Stevensons: left to right, Eliza Fell Davis, Elizabeth Stevenson Ives (the Governor's sister), Helen Davis Stevenson (his mother) and Hester Brown Fell, his great-grandmother.

Lewis Green Stevenson lived up to the family tradition by being a war correspondent, mine manager for Mrs. Phoebe Hearst, Illinois Secretary of State and vice-presidential possibility in 1924.

Helen Davis Stevenson, daughter of W. O. Davis, helped form her son's literary tastes by reading him Scott, Dickens, Thackeray and Greek mythology.

Governor Stevenson inspects framed copy of three-page autobiography written by Lincoln at the request of Jesse W. Fell. Original manuscript, given to Fell, is now in Library of Congress.

Lincoln rewarded Fell for assistance in the early years of his career by making him a paymaster in the Union Army. Fell and Lincoln first met in 1835.

something you don't decline — that it transcends any other obligation. I thought that carried weight. So did the argument that this election is of frightening importance, particularly to our foreign policy. You just can't fight for a lot of things that I have fought for and then not be in the battle when they ring the bell.

"Then, a lot of people seemed to think I was calculating on the basis of its being a bad political year. That irked me. People would say 'Governor, you could win' not 'Governor, you should run,' assuming that I was being motivated by the possibility of victory.

"Well anyway, I'm afraid I'm making it all very complex. You can just boil it down to the ideas that I tried to say concisely in the statement I wrote. I just meant to keep my commitments to my friends and followers in Illinois and finish the work we have started. Illinois means a great deal to me. My family have lived and flourished here for over a hundred years. I'll be content if I can leave the state government a lot better than I found it and I think I can."

While Stevenson's official statement was about as clear a declaration of intentions as could have been hoped for, two questions, in the nature of things, remained unanswered by it. One was whether under the circumstances his party would accept it at face value. The answer to this appeared to be "no," for a "draft Stevenson" movement started the day after it was issued, and when Stevenson spoke in New York at a testimonial dinner to Averill Harriman, he received more applause than the four avowed candidates present put together, including the guest of honor. The other question, even if the party did accept it, was where it left Stevenson.

Ordinarily, a defeated presidential candidate — and it seemed fairly sure that any Democratic candidate except Stevenson would be a defeated one in 1952 — heads the party until the next national convention; but this is on the assumption that the nominee is the party's strongest available personage, which, if Stevenson failed to run, would clearly not be the case. One thing at least seemed clear. That was that whatever happened at the convention, Stevenson would be the Number One Democrat in the U. S. and a major voice in the councils of the nation for many years to come.

Meanwhile, if one test of presidential caliber is the ability to stay calm under pressure, Stevenson's reaction to the commotion rated better than passing marks. On the way back to Springfield from the Jefferson-Jackson Day dinner, the Governor stopped off to look over a state mental hospital at Manteno, Illinois, and a group of the inmates cheered him as "Mr. President." "I didn't know," said Stevenson later, "whether it was a case of extreme psychosis, or whether I should have been flattered."

When the mansion quota of visiting newspapermen jumped from one or two a week to a dozen or so a day, many of whom spent their time interviewing each other in the basement hall, Stevenson remarked: "I ran out of words trying to be witty. . . . I usually try to say the same thing — about how I am running for Governor of Illinois and nothing else, and that I like the work and love Illinois — but sometimes I find that I just smile like a mental defective."

A climax of some sort was capped when, in the midst of all the uproar, a biographer approached the Governor and announced that he was going to write a book about him. Stevenson's poise, as usual, was equal to the occasion.

"I don't see how you're going to do it," said the Governor. "My life has been hopelessly undramatic. I wasn't born in a log cabin. I didn't work my way through school nor did I rise from rags to riches, and there's no use trying to pretend I did. I'm not a Willkie and I don't claim to be a simple, barefoot La Salle Street lawyer. You might be able to write about some of my ancestors. They accomplished quite a lot at one time or another but you can't do anything much about me. At least, I'd hate to have to try it."

3

STEVENSON's belief that his ancestors might provide material for a book is amply justified; so amply, indeed, that the book would have to be in several volumes, preferably written by Parkman, Fiske or some similar historian capable of taking a long view with a panoramic lens. Eight of the great-great-great-great-great grandparents of the Governor were among the first settlers of Virginia and North Carolina. Their descendants and those of the one hundred and twenty other members of his eighth generation forebears have been involved in so many noteworthy episodes in so many different parts of the country that it sometimes begins to seem as though United States history were merely a footnote to the history of the united, or at least related, Stevensons — not to mention the Osbornes, Greens, Fells, Brevards, Davises and Willises, who were also included in the acts.

To go back toward the colonial beginning, when Colonel Henry Willis was founding Fredericksburg, Virginia, would widen the scope of investigation beyond reasonable bounds. A better starting point might be Colonel Joshua Fry, a comparatively recent example of a Stevenson ancestor, who was merely one of the Governor's great-great-great-grandparents on the maternal side. The Colonel, unlike the Governor, *did* graduate from Oxford, an accomplishment which, in his time, was not regarded as a barrier to leadership in the U. S. He then emigrated to Virginia around 1750, taught Mathematics at William and Mary College, collaborated with Thomas Jefferson's father, Peter, on the first accurate map of "Inhabited Parts of Virginia" and got his army rank from King George III who commissioned him to lead colonial troops against the French at Fort Duquesne, now Pittsburgh. En route to the battle, the Colonel fell ill and died, after handing over his sword to a twenty-two-year-old lieutenant who took command of the troops and buried his superior under a marker inscribed: "Under this tree lies the body of the good, the just and noble Fry."

The lieutenant, as was not at all surprising under the circumstances, was George Washington. Washington had not then quite achieved membership in the Stevenson family but he got into it later on, not once but twice, through his grandfather Lawrence, two of whose granddaughters by Mildred Washington Gregory Willis eventually became Stevenson greats to the third and fourth power respectively.

Since anyone who knew the names of enough progenitors to a sufficient coefficient of greats could prove some degree of kinship with everyone else in the world either living or dead, little would be gained by trying to cover all the stratifications of U. S. history and geography encompassed by earlier Stevenson progenitors. What is more to the point is that, in Stevenson's case, when the family circle is narrowed down to comparatively recent times and thus numerically reduced, the ancestral role in national affairs becomes more noticeable rather than less so, as in the case of the Governor's mere great-grandfather on his mother's side, Jesse W. Fell. Fell was a peripatetic Quaker who, starting out on foot at twenty from New Garden, Chester County, Pennsylvania, soon covered enough ground, literally as well as metaphorically, to provide material for a pocket-sized Atlas as well as a history of his era, instead of just a bedroom portrait.

After pausing for a year in what was then Wheeling, Virginia, to run an Abolitionist newspaper, and for two more in Steubenville, Ohio, to take a law degree, Fell wandered into Illinois where, having inspected Danville, Springfield, New Salem, Decatur, Jacksonville, Pekin and Delavan, he lit, temporarily, in Bloomington, which has been the citadel of his descendants ever since. In Bloomington, of which the population then was under a hundred, Fell augmented his income from the law by numerous sidelines. These included real estate, politics, literature, education and botany, which he practiced after the fashion of Johnny Appleseed, for whom he may indeed have been a model.

In addition to becoming Bloomington's first lawyer, Fell became its first newspaper proprietor by starting "The Bloomington Observer and McLean County Advocate," using presses and type that had been shipped up the Mississippi and hauled overland from Pekin. The paper folded after twenty issues, but Fell subsequently started several others and became a contributor to the Chicago *Tribune*. When not founding papers, Fell was founding towns, which included Pontiac, Clinton, Towanda, Lexington, Le Roy, El Paso and way stops, in most of which he also acquired substantial real estate holdings. He also started schools and colleges like the Normal University near Bloomington, to an offshoot of which Adlai Stevenson was sent, with indifferent results, in 1915.

In the course of his law practice in Bloomington, Fell found himself obliged, in the winter of 1834-35, to go to Vandalia, then the state capital, to battle a bill under legislative consideration to reduce the size of McLean County. In Vandalia he lived in a boarding house at which one of the other guests was a young member of the General Assembly whose name was, naturally, Abraham Lincoln. Friendship between Fell and Lincoln ripened rapidly. By 1854, when Senator Stephen Douglas came to Bloomington to make a speech, it was not only characteristic for him to discuss this project with Fell but also characteristic of Fell to suggest that he share the platform with the then obscure Emancipator. Douglas declined the invitation but took a raincheck. Four years later, when Lincoln was running for the Senate, he accepted it, in what developed into the famous series of Lincoln-Douglas debates, which lead eventually to Lincoln's nomination for the presidency.

Lincoln's nomination was not his only debt to Fell. Like Stevenson in early 1952, Lincoln, in 1858, was still unknown to the rest of the country, especially the East. Fell pestered him to remedy this situation by writing an autobiography, which Lincoln eventually dashed off in three pages. As the first, shortest and most authentic of the several hundred lives of Lincoln later composed, as well as the only one in the subject's own handwriting, this biography, of which Lincoln gave Fell the only copy, served its immediate purpose of helping him win the campaign of 1860. As one of the most precious items of Lincolniana in existence, it also later on served the additional purpose of getting Adlai Stevenson involved in politics for the first time, in 1936.

That the Lincoln autobiography figured in Stevenson's career was due to his predecessor in the Executive Mansion, Henry Horner, who served as Governor from 1932 to 1940, when he died just before his second term expired. Horner was an ardent collector of Lincolniana. When he and Stevenson met from time to time in Chicago, Horner often inquired about the wherabouts of the famous manuscript. He wanted to raise a fund to buy it for $50,000 and give it to the state library before it was acquired by the Library of Congress, which, in fact, eventually got it as a gift. Stevenson explained that the manuscript was in the possession of two elderly great-aunts, then living modestly in Los Gatos, California, who were Fell's surviving daughters. His extreme disinterest in profiting from the family's possession of this valuable relic made a deep impression upon the Governor. It lead to an acquaintance and then a friendship between Stevenson and Horner which culminated in Horner asking Stevenson to be the treasurer of his campaign fund in 1936, an honor which, though Stevenson declined it, was his own first practical contact with politics.

While Jesse Fell's career was lively enough to provide material for a biography by Francis Milton I. Moorehouse, published by the University of Illinois in 1916, he was by no means the star performer in the large cast of Stevenson ancestors. In fact much of the data about him is included in another book by an ancestor with a better claim to such billing. This was the first Adlai Ewing Stevenson, nicknamed "the Headsman," whose son married Fell's grand-daughter, Helen Davis. Although he was Fell's junior by almost a generation, Stevenson was well acquainted with both Fell and Lincoln and recorded some of their doings in his book of memoirs, *Something of Men I Have Known,* published in 1909. In these memoirs however, Lincoln and Fell are merely curtain raisers to Stevenson's own career, which excelled the family's already lofty standard in such matters.

The first Adlai Stevenson got his Christian name from his great-great-grandfather, Adlai Osborne. Where Adlai Osborne got it is no mystery either since it occurs only once in world literature, and there inconsequentially, in the twenty-ninth verse of the first chapter of the Book of Chronicles which, for no apparent reason, identifies someone named "Shapat," inadequately enough, as being "the son of Adlai." *Why* he got it remains a riddle. Grounds for the supposition that "Adlai" means "the Just" or indeed, anything else, are extremely dubious. A more plausible surmise may be that Osborne's Scotch Presbyterian forebears hoped that in the course of searching through the Good Book for its lone reference to his namesake, their offspring would acquire a taste for improving literature.

The first Adlai Stevenson's nickname provides less of an enigma. This he got for lopping no fewer than forty thousand Republican postmasters off the federal payroll when, having served two creditable terms in Congress, he was appointed Assistant Postmaster General by Grover Cleveland in 1884. Since the Republicans had been in power ever since the Civil War and were almost as long overdue for a thorough pruning as the Truman administration is sometimes thought to be at present, Adlai Stevenson's mass severances are readily understandable although, save on grounds of economy, they might seem unjustifiable to his grandson, an advocate of civil service and the merit system for government employees. To Cleveland they seemed not only justifiable but praiseworthy. Adlai Stevenson was rewarded, in addition to his nickname, with the vice-presidency in 1892, when Cleveland got elected for the second time.

The present Adlai Stevenson's grandfather was a kindly gregarious, indefatigable public servant whose large stock of public esteem and stamina enabled him to run for office twice more, once when he was defeated for Vice-President on the Bryan ticket in 1900, and again when at seventy-three, he was defeated for the governorship of Illinois in 1908 by a mere 23,000 votes to the national ticket's 179,000. For sheer durability, however, he was outclassed by his wife, whose pioneer heritage cropped out in the field of womens' clubs. Mrs. Letitia Green Stevenson was the second President General of the National Society of the Daughters of the American Revolution and served four terms as such, from 1893 to 1898, during which the organization grew from 2,760 to 23,097, and got started on its rise to nationwide importance. She was also a pioneer Colonial Dame and a pioneer member of the group which met in Washington in 1896 to found the Congress of Mothers, which later became the Parent-Teacher Association. When the Illinois Congress of Mothers was organized in 1900, she promptly became one of its vice presidents and was still serving it thus in an honorary capacity two years after her husband had settled

down to view his long and dazzling career in literary retro-
spect.

The rendezvous with history of Lewis Green Stevenson,
father of Adlai II and son of Adlai I, was delayed by tuberculosis of a shoulder bone, in consequence of a youthful
shooting accident. Before his marriage to Jesse Fell's grand-
daughter, whose father owned a newspaper named the
Bloomington *Pantagraph,* itself descended from the original
Fell publications, young Stevenson went to China and Japan
to cover the war in which Japan acquired Korea, starting
the still widening spiral of misery for that nation, about
which his son was to write a half-century later. After the
war, he and his wife and their infant daughter went to
Arizona for the climate. Also in Arizona, for different reasons,
was Mrs. Phoebe Apperson Hearst, who had inherited several
gold and copper mines from her husband, Senator George
Hearst, father of the late William Randolph. Senator Hearst
had of course been a great Washington friend of Adlai
Stevenson I. His widow hastened to befriend the latter's
son, by hiring him to manage her mines. When young
Hearst contracted the habit of starting newspapers, young
Lewis Stevenson transferred his interest to those and became
assistant business manager of the brand new *Examiner* in
Los Angeles, where Adlai Stevenson was born in the historic
year of 1900.

After serving as his father's private secretary in the campaign of the fall of that year, Lewis Stevenson returned to
Bloomington and directed his managerial talents first to agriculture, as represented by forty-nine farms comprising 12,000

acres in Illinois, Indiana and Iowa, and then into politics, as represented by his father's gubernatorial campaign of 1908. His own first public office was that of Secretary of State of Illinois, in 1914. In the world war that started that year he conducted special investigations mostly relating to coal and fuel supplies for the Navy Department under an appointment by President Wilson. His own contacts with the presidency were tangential. They occurred in 1924 when, as a delegate to the marathon Democratic convention which chose John W. Davis, he nominated David F. Houston, and in 1928, when he himself was widely mentioned as a possible running mate for Al Smith.

To suppose that the plethora of distinguished Stevenson progenitors would be balanced by a dearth of distinguished contemporary relatives would be a *non sequitur* of monstrous proportions. Genealogical tables show, on the contrary, that Stevenson is distantly related not only to Vice-President Alben Barkley, whose grandmother was the Headsman's first cousin, but also to Georgia's Senator Richard Russell, who might have been his own running mate this year. The relationship in the latter case was discovered during the war in an interchange of correspondence between the two on the subject of Dr. Ephraim Brevard, who proved to be their mutual great-great-great uncle. Brevard was a miner notable among Stevenson's forebears whose chief claim to fame was the Mecklenberg Declaration of Independence, whereby Mecklenberg County, North Carolina declared its independence from the British Crown sometime before the thirteen colonies followed suit.

The only task more onerous than really tracing the history

of Adlai Stevenson II might be tracing that of his children, since this would also involve the family tree of the Governor's former wife. The branch of the Borden clan to which Mrs. Stevenson belongs is not, as has been frequently asserted, the one that founded the milk company. Her father, a socialite and financier who made the first of several fortunes as a colleague of John Hertz in the Yellow Cab Company, is presently active in mining near St. Louis but the Bordens may also have enough other connections with history to outclass the Stevensons, as a single case in point may adequately show.

Mrs. Stevenson's aunt is Mary Borden, a novelist now resident in England, whose novel, *You the Jury*, about the trial of Christ, is a Book of the Month Club choice in both England and the U. S. Mary Borden lives in England because she is married to Sir Louis Spears, renowned there as a diplomat, soldier, politician and historian of his confreres in such fields. Spears wears on his watch chain not a spare watch, like Stevenson, but a little heraldic lion, in a reclining posture. This lion was given to one of his ancestors by the Black Prince at the Battle of Poitiers in 1356. When the French Knights charged in that highly decisive engagement, Irish swordsmen lying in long grass in front of the British bowmen rose up suddenly to hamstring the French horses as they charged over them. The *lion couchant* was one of four which the Prince, resting after the battle, impulsively wrenched off the knuckles of his left gauntlet and tossed to the captains who had contributed most to his victory as mementoes of their crucial feat. The lions on the Prince's right gauntlet are still attached to it and on display in the Tower of London, along with the rest of the famous armor he wore that day.

The Black Prince's lion, comparable to Lincoln's auto-biography as a British keepsake, has also had contemporary connotations. In 1917, when he quit the cabinet to go to France as a major of infantry, Winston Churchill liked it so much that he borrowed it from his friend, General Spears to carry as a good luck charm. It proved so useful as such that he kept it for four years and only gave it back on the assurance that he could have it again if an occasion of need arose. During the last war, in which Churchill sent Spears to escort General de Gaulle out of France after the fall of Paris, the occasion came when the Prime Minister caught pneu-monia in North Africa. Lying, as he thought, near death, he sent for the lion. This time, Spears, who was the British Minister in Beirut at the time, got it back more promptly from a messenger who arrived by plane with a note of thanks from Churchill to the effect that it had again served him well.

If America, to the horror of Colonel McCormick, were a country like England, where titles are awarded for meritor-ious service to the state, Stevenson's lineage, like Churchill's, would doubtless be dotted by peerages. Although not disting-uished by such accolades, U. S. families like the Stevensons, Lodges, Roosevelts, Adamses and even Tafts supply valuable material for the sociologists. Two schools of thought exist about them. One school suggests that their prowess is due mainly to heredity and that their virtues are handed down via the glands, the bony structure and the blood stream. The other school suggests that their prowess is due mainly to environment, since good parents raise their children properly and famous forebears set them lofty standards to maintain or elevate.

In the case of Stevenson, ample evidence exists to provide argument for either side. On the one hand, since all of the Governor's traits, including most notably his partiality for travel, politics, agronomy, and being at the center of things, have been conspicuously displayed by one or more of his forebears, he may well have inherited them. On the other hand, since anything Stevenson reads or any place he visits inside or even outside the U. S., is likely to have some link with his progenitors, they have also been an omnipresent environmental influence. Nonetheless, while even a cursory glance at the evidence is sufficient to substantiate Stevenson's belief that his ancestors were a lively group, the Governor's notion that his own career has been hopelessly undramatic will bear much closer scrutiny.

4

O NE DRAMATIC event in the life of Adlai Stevenson was
an accident on the evening of December 30th, 1912, which
resulted in the death of his fifteen-year-old cousin-by-mar-
riage, Ruth Mary Merwin.

The accident was tragic for all concerned. To understand
why it was especially so for Stevenson it is necessary to know
something about the circumstances.

When Adlai Stevenson was born, his sister Elizabeth,
called Buffie in the family, had already been on the scene
for over two years. According to the psychologists, second
children often consider themselves to be family interlopers,
obliged to justify their presence by especially good behavior.
In the case of Adlai, there were no subsequent arrivals to
diminish this illusion. Being a serious and sensitive child,
he endeared himself to everyone by excellent deportment.
When, on rare occasions, his conduct left something to be
desired, he was more upset by it than anyone.

Adlai's grandfather Davis gave him a red-handled jack
knife. A few days later, Adlai mislaid it. His grandfather
found it. Thinking to teach his grandson a gentle lesson in
prudence, he asked him at lunch whether he liked his new
knife.

"I've lost it," said Adlai, and broke into tears of remorse
before his grandfather could fish the knife out of his pocket.

On another occasion, Stevenson, like countless small boys before him, yanked a table cloth, causing some china to fall and break. In this instance, his self-reproach was even more acute than it had been in that of the knife. He retreated to a dog-kennel where his worried parents discovered him several hours later, sleeping on the straw.

There is, of course, nothing much for a Parson Weems in incidents like this. Oldest children, only children and children in large families all have certain behavior traits in common. Second children in families of two are no exceptions in this respect. However, that young Stevenson had a well-developed, not to say precocious, conscience bears on the later incident in question.

What happened on that Christmas holiday evening was that his sister Buffie, who felt as protective about Adlai as he felt admiring of her, had been given permission by her parents to have a few of her friends for supper. It was to be a teen-age party. Mr. and Mrs. Stevenson went out to call on neighbors. Adlai Stevenson had his supper early but was allowed to join his elders later.

One of the boys present was a student at a military academy. After dinner, it was suggested that he entertain the others by going through the manual of arms. Adlai was sent to get a twenty-two rifle. The military academy student examined the gun carefully, to make sure that there were no bullets in the barrel or the magazine. Then he executed the manual of arms, to the applause of everyone. Adlai was given the gun to hold. He tried to copy the motions of his sister's friend. It was at this moment that the gun went off. Later investigation showed that one shell in the gun —

perhaps because of a rusty spring in the ejecting mechanism — had failed to emerge in the pre-drill inspection. During the manual of arms the gun had been shaken and the stock thumped on in the floor. This had loosened the spring and released the bullet. Thus, by the time Adlai got the gun in his hands, through no fault whatsoever upon his part, it had become a lethal weapon.

The bullet entered Ruth Merwin's forehead. She fell dead, on the carpet in the hall. The elder Stevensons returned a few minutes later.

"What boy did this?" Lewis Stevenson asked.

"I did," said Adlai. Then he went up to his room and lay down on the bed.

At an inquest the next day, he was cleared of all blame for the accident. The account of the inquest published in the *Pantagraph* mentioned that "Adlai Stevenson, prostrated with grief, was unable to be present."

What effect the accident in 1912 had upon Adlai Stevenson's character is a matter of surmise. But between the time it happened and the winter of 1952, no one spoke of it to him, and he spoke of it to no one. This was established by William Glasgow, the *Time* correspondent who prepared the research for the cover story — in which the accident was not mentioned. In Bloomington, Glasgow heard rumors that the governor had once been involved in some sort of mysterious mishap. He expected to get details from the Governor's close friends in Chicago. None of them had ever heard of the affair. He made further inquiries in Bloomington and finally read the account of the accident in the *Pantagraph*. Glasgow felt hesitant about questioning the Governor on the subject but finally told him what he had heard and said that he needed to know all the facts.

"Stevenson," Glasgow said recently, "looked away for a moment and then said: 'You know you are the first person who has talked to me about that since it happened — and this is the first time I have spoken of it to anyone' I asked the Governor whether he minded telling me the story. 'No,' said Stevenson, 'I'll tell you everything I can remember about it.' Then he told me the whole story, in a matter of fact way."

The Governor told the story substantially as it has been related here.

Before the accident, Stevenson had spent most of his winters in the South with his mother and his delicate and aging grandfather Davis. Summers were spent at the rambling old Davis house at the lake resort of Charlevoix, Michigan. Davis was a Quaker who had come out west as a young man and landed in Bloomington. When Lincoln made Fell a paymaster in the Union Army, Fell took Davis south with him as his clerk; and Davis later married Fell's daughter, Eliza. After the war, he bought and built up the Bloomington *Pantagraph* (meaning "Write everything"). A great admirer of Robert Burns, Davis read his poems to his grandson as soon as the latter was capable of understanding human speech, and followed them up with selections from Bret Harte and Lewis Carroll. The Stevenson grandparents also summered at Charlevoix. They were a more formidable couple, who called each other "Mr." and "Mrs." and were regularly called on by notables like William Jennings Bryan, when they passed through that part of the land. Young Stevenson often called on them also and formed an early taste for associating with the great and near great.

Lewis Stevenson was a health addict who invented a soya bean coffee substitute, excercised with dumb-bells and fed his children orange juice, then a dietary rarity. Mrs. Stevenson was a fond mother. Her pet name for her son, made partly by switching one of the consonants in his real one, was "Laddie." She, too, provided copious readings from Scott, Dickens and Thackeray and gave him lessons at home until he was nine. When he finally got to school, he was thus a newcomer to a previously integrated group and, as such, obliged to fight for rank. In 1912, the Stevensons spent a year in Switzerland where the children attended a school in Lausanne. There, as a newcomer who did not even know the language in which the lessons were given, he found himself in an intensified version of the same position.

After finishing grade school in Bloomington, young Adlai was sent to the high school at Bloomington's twin town of Normal, which functioned as a sort of practice field for the teachers attending the State Normal University founded by his great-grandfather Fell. At Normal, Stevenson was preparing to enter Princeton, which he had selected as an alma mater for family reasons. Adlai Osborne had graduated there in 1768. Its Theological Seminary had also been attended by his great grandfather Dr. Lewis Warner Green, a famous nineteenth-century pedagogue and Kentucky liberal, who freed his numerous slaves as soon as he inherited them and served as president of several Presbyterian institutions including Centre College, Kentucky, of whose first graduating class he had been one of the two members. The efforts of the Fell academy to enable young Stevenson to matriculate at Princeton were a lamentable failure. The sum of Stevenson's marks in his first three college board examinations was insufficient to have given him a passing grade in any one of them. His father concluded that Normal was a misnomer either for the school or for his son and sent the latter off to Choate, an Eastern preparatory institution noted for its high scholastic standards.

At Choate, cast in his customary role of late-coming stranger, Stevenson, who had already acquired the family knack for writing generally, and, for reporting in particular, quickly observed that the road to renown lay not in further fisticuffs but in heeling the Choate *News,* an unusually handsome and *Pantagraph*-like prep-school journal. He "heeled" the board, made the paper and was elected editor-in-chief and president of his class for what should have been his third and final year. By this time, however, the U. S. had entered World War I and Choate sixth formers were scampering off to enlist. Stevenson finished the school year of 1918 and then enlisted in the United States Naval Reserve unit at Princeton.

In the first world war, the shortage of naval personnel was less acute than in World War II but the shortage of ships was more acute. At landlocked Princeton, Stevenson put in most of his time marching up and down Nassau Street with his fellow apprentice seamen, learning the nautical terms for floors, doors and stairways, and rowing up and down Carnegie Lake in a whaleboat. Even the whaleboats were in short supply and some seamen had to sit on the bank. While

there, lest any of their time be wasted, an admiral who had
sailed in wooden ships taught them to tie knots in rope.
Before they got a chance to utilize these skills, hostilities
had ended.

What the Choate *News* is to Choate and the *Pantagraph*
to Bloomington, the *Daily Princetonian* is to Princeton.
Stevenson competed for a position on the board in his sopho-
more year, won it in the first competition and eventually
became the paper's managing editor, as well as an elected
member of the senior council. In the senior poll for "Biggest
Politician," he placed third. Instead of fraternities or secret
societies, Princeton has eating clubs for upperclassmen. Along
with several of his fellow Princetonian board members,
Stevenson joined Quadrangle, generally considered one of
the best. In the relaxed twenties, Princetonian academic
convention called for getting what was called "a gentleman's
third group," i.e., passing marks. In his studies, principally
English and U. S., or family, history, Stevenson subscribed
to it. According to *Time,* meek demeanor caused him to get
the nickname of "Rabbit." According to Stevenson, Rabbit
was less a genuine nickname than an insulting appellation
applied to him by his room-mates, William Ellery Hale and
H. Hamilton Hackney, because of his enthusiastic manner of
devouring lettuce, carrots, celery and other garden provender.
Of the two explanations, the Governor's is more plausible.
When eating a forkful of salad, Stevenson still has a distinctly
leporine look. His eyes bulge, his jaws work rapidly, his nose
twitches and his ears wiggle slightly. Stevenson's favorite
rabbit food is the tomato. The Governor likes tomatoes so
much that whenever possible he eats them boiled, broiled or

stewed for lunch, dinner or both every day and sometimes for breakfast also, in addition to using copious helpings of ketchup as a relish, washed down with a sort of highball made of tomato juice and yogurt.

Another frequent canard about Stevenson's education is that he flunked out of Harvard Law School. What really happened was more complicated. During school and college vacations Stevenson had made several trips to Europe with his family or classmates and two trips to the far West. After his last year at Princeton, he and a classmate named Ralph Goodwin drove in the latter's Jordan roadster to spend another summer on a ranch in Wyoming. Ranch life proved much to their liking. Stevenson and Goodwin decided to stay on in the West, began looking at property and presently found some they thought would suit them. When Stevenson wrote to tell his father of the new turn his career had taken, Lewis Stevenson failed to cooperate. He replied that if Stevenson did not report back on time to attend Harvard Law School, someone would come to fetch him. At Harvard Law School, Stevenson got passing marks but, unlike the later generation of embryo New Dealers who sat mesmerized by the pedagogic wizardry of the renowned Felix Frankfurter, Stevenson never met Frankfurter and never put his heart in it. After his second year at Harvard, the death of one of his uncles posed a practical legal problem which gave Stevenson a valid excuse for playing truant from the law school.

The will of Stevenson's Grandfather Davis had provided that the shares in the *Pantagraph* be held in life estate by his children and then divided between their children, of whom there were five. Two were Adlai Stevenson and his sister. The other three were their Merwin cousins, cousins also of Ruth Mary Merwin who, however, had not been a Davis grandchild. Helen Davis Stevenson's brother, Hibbard O. Davis, had managed the Pantagraph since their father's death in 1911. Hibbard Davis's death however raised the question of whether Mrs. Stevenson and her sister Mrs. Merwin should inherit equal shares, which would have given the two Stevenson heirs as much as the three Merwins, or whether each grandchild was to receive an equal share, which would have meant that the three Merwins got sixty percent and the two Stevensons forty. At a family conclave it was decided to institute a friendly suit to settle the matter. Pending the outcome of the suit, young Stevenson and his cousin, Davis C. Merwin could learn about running the paper, on the editorial and business side respectively.

Stevenson spent a couple of years on the paper in various editorial capacities but, by the time the courts ruled that the Stevenson and Merwin families should have equal shares of the ownership, his interest in becoming a newspaper editor had waned. He decided to finish up his law course and, having fallen a year behind his classmates who had already graduated from Harvard, he entered the law school at Northwestern University and took his degree there in 1926. Another cousin, Loring Merwin, still runs the Pantagraph, along independent Republican lines. Stevenson still owns roughly twenty-five percent of the company but resigned as a director and vice President after being elected Governor.

Confronted by the fact that his formal schooling was definitely over, Stevenson decided to have a last look at Europe before settling down to practice law in Chicago. Starting with Switzerland, which had opened his eyes to the pleasurable benefits of travel, he had by now covered most of the beaten tracks from Scandinavia to the toe of Italy. He wanted to go somewhere new, and hit on Russia. Foreign visitors to the Soviet Union were not then being welcomed by the Intourist plan installed in the thirties. In order to effect an entry, Stevenson got Hearst INS and *Pantagraph* credentials as a foreign correspondent. He planned to get a great scoop by interviewing Finance Minister Chicherin on the subject of the then highly controversial New Economic Policy. Chicherin was a clamlike ex-diplomat who had proved immune to the blandishments of more experienced foreign correspondents. Stevenson thought he might loosen up for a young novice who had come all the way from Chicago.

The first thing Stevenson needed was a visa. In Washington the Russian embassy said this would take time. He could pick it up in London. In London, the visa was not ready. He was told to pick it up in Paris. Paris said Vienna: Vienna said Belgrade. Belgrade said Budapest. Budapest said Bucharest. Bucharest said Constantinople. In Constantinople, Stevenson went to the consulate for eight days in a row. Each day he heard that there was no news about the visa. On the ninth day he went sightseeing. On the tenth day he went back to the consulate. "Where have you been?" asked the Russian consul. "We have been looking for you. Here is your visa."

Equipped with a visa, the next problem was to get to Moscow. By bribing a boatman to row him out to its anchorage, Stevenson managed to scramble on board an ancient Italian freighter which was just leaving the harbor. His cabin mate was an aging Italian diplomat who passed the time shooting at seagulls from a deck chair on the stern. At Batum, all Stevenson's books, including Bernard Pares' Russian history were confiscated and the diplomat helped him catch a train for Tiflis. From Tiflis, he made his way to Baku. At Baku, he boarded a *wagon-lit* for Moscow, via Kiev and Rostov. This time his room-mate was a bushy-bearded Bolshevik with whom he passed nine intimate days without exchanging a syllable.

Having arrived in Moscow, where the first thing he noticed were homeless children fighting to lick the cobblestones where someone had spilled some jam, Stevenson presented himself at the Foreign Office and explained his mission. He was told to come back the next morning. The next morning he presented himself again. He was told to come back the next morning. This continued for four weeks during which Stevenson passed his afternoons in less monotonous fashion. He lived in a house run by two middle-aged Quaker ladies which was also a favorite meeting place for members of the correspondents' colony. This included the late H. R. Knicker-bocker on his first assignment, Junius Wood of the Chicago *News* and Walter Duranty of the New York *Times,* then at the outset of his notable career. Stevenson roamed about town with them and called on surviving relatives of some White Russian émigrés whom he had known in Chicago.

One of Stevenson's Chicago Russian friends was Prince Nicholas Galitzine whose sister later became Mrs. Lester Armour. Galitzine had asked him to look up his aunt, the

Countess Anastasia Galitzine, who had been a lady-in-waiting at the court of the last Czarina. Stevenson did so and found the countess in a fifth-floor room of a run-down tenement where she shared a bathroom with a score of other tenants. Stevenson's visit put her life in jeopardy but she was glad to see him notwithstanding. She greeted him in English, acquired from her governess, with an apology for her costume, a court dress with leg-of-mutton sleeves, dating from the Edwardian era. "Please excuse these rags," said the Countess, "I am getting to the bottom of my trunk."

Unlike Stevenson's visa, his appointment with Chicherin was never forthcoming. After a month of daily calls at the Foreign Office, he left without it but with a twenty-five year start on many of his later colleagues in the diplomatic world, insofar as intimate, first-hand knowledge of Soviet Russia was concerned. This knowledge stood Stevenson in good stead in 1946 when he was largely responsible for running the United Nations Preparatory Commission meeting in London. His job called for frequent talks with Gromyko who perhaps felt that Stevenson's sophistication about conditions in Russia, gave them a common bond. They became so friendly that Gromyko even came to dine at Stevenson's house and exchanged repartee with him. Stevenson made a speech in which he said that if one compared the U. N. to a baby born in San Francisco, then the object of the London meeting was to provide it with clothes and equipment.

"One question," said Gromyko, "When does the baby get the teeth?"

5

ACCORDING to popular theory, U. S. presidents start at the bottom of the social and economic ladder and clamber to the top by sheer ability. This theory is pleasing but untenable. A few presidents like Jackson, Lincoln and Truman lacked early environmental advantages. They are exceptions who prove the rule, exemplified by most of the others, that presidents spring from the mansion rather than the modest cottage.

To conclude that this makes the ascent an easy one would, of course, also be unwarranted. People who start at the bottom of the social ladder attract much favorable notice when they climb up a rung or two. People who start near the top or even half way up usually have to descend before they can even start to climb. Even after climbing quite a distance, they only get back where they started — not a feat to summon much applause. A young man who bears the name of celebrated forebears is at a further disadvantage. It took Franklin Roosevelt two decades to live down his distant kinship with Theodore. As for Theodore Roosevelt's own son and namesake, the late Theodore Jr., he was tripped at the outset by a famous Rollin Kirby cartoon which appeared when he ran for the governorship of New York in 1924. This showed huge pits made by a pair of seven-league boots crossing the sands of time. Theodore Jr. was a midget, lost in one of the pits. The caption said: "Following his father's footsteps."

In addition to the handicap of a well-known name, Stevenson had inherited another one. Lewis Stevenson was a Presbyterian Democrat. As though this were an insufficiently contradictory mixture, his wife came from a family of Unitarian Republicans. Their marriage — the most spectacular Bloomington social event of its year — had been made even more notable by its Montague-Capulet politico-religious aspects. Stevenson, who says, "I was a compromise from the outset," had been brought up in his mother's faith and his father's party. His path in Chicago's business world might have been smoother had the process been reversed. Most of the nation's top business communities are strongly pro-Republican. Chicago's, whose thinking is dominated by the *Tribune,* is more so than most. Stevenson's position in 1927 when he joined the city's oldest law firm, Cutting, Moore and Sidley, was that of a one-man ideological Fifth Column.

Fortunately for Stevenson, politics did not count for much in 1927 — though even if they had, his temperament might have enabled him to profit from a situation which was in some ways analogous to the one he had encountered often in his school days. Under the pressure of new and adverse circumstances, his conscience, always reasonably clear, now began to shine like a mirror. He worked a sixty-hour, forty-dollar week, and his personality expanded, prompting him to take a lively part in the lively social doings of the era. Ellen Borden was one of the most eminently marriageable, as well as one of the most attractive young ladies on the Chicago social scene. Her wedding to Stevenson in December 1928 was one of the top events of that Chicago season.

The causes of the Stevensons' divorce in 1949 while somewhat puzzling, appear to derive chiefly from incompatibility due to increasingly divergent interests. Mrs. Stevenson's tastes lie in the world of art and literature. While Eastern politicoes were trying unsuccessfully to get Stevenson to Washington last April, Mrs. Stevenson was in Washington trying successfully to get Dylan Thomas, the Welsh poet, to visit Chicago, where Thomas gave a reading in the Arts Club lounge. When Mrs. Stevenson got her divorce in Las Vegas a year after her husband's election the stated reason was that she disliked public life. This was a simplification but perhaps an adequate one. No other persons, and no scandal whatsoever, affected the legal proceedings. Stevenson, who opposes divorce generally, was shocked and saddened but not surprised. The divorce, accompanied by a substantial settlement, was handled without rancor or undue publicity. It had been preceded by twenty years of apparently happy marriage.

At Cutting, Moore and Sidley, a conservative firm engaged in a corporate and general practice which included almost everything except divorces, criminal trials, and patents, Stevenson got a good all-around look at the U. S. economy from a backstage seat. In the late nineteen-twenties, when he was in legal slang "carrying books for the senior partners," the firm's work often concerned the preparation of new issues of securities, which were then being gobbled up faster than they could be put on the market. After his father's death early in 1929, Stevenson had a modest capital with which

to participate cautiously in the national mania for speculation. In due course, he lost most of his profits but the firm
was kept even busier than before, in efforts to repair or
disassemble the wreckage of financial structures it had helped
to build.

Illinois was one of the U. S. states hardest hit by the
Depression. Where Easterners had concentrated on common
stocks, Mid-Westerners had always invested heavily in farm
mortgages. When the bottom dropped out of everything, it
expropriated not only the mortgagees but also the mortgage-
holders. The major single catastrophe in Chicago's urban
financial world was the thunderous collapse of Samuel
Insull's utility and holding companies. Like many other
Chicago law firms, Stevenson's was called upon to help pick
up the pieces. Salvage jobs on farm mortgages and urban
bond issues gave Stevenson an all-around inside familiarity
with the Depression and its causes. Its consequences were
spectacularly evident from his window on La Salle Street,
in the breadlines and the swarms of unemployed and homeless, sleeping under bridges.

In managing numerous farms in three states, Stevenson's
father had had control of what amounted to a miniature
department of agriculture. His methods, if not actually experimental, were progressive and advanced. He tinkered with
new kinds of crop rótation, grew huge quantities of soy-
beans, and enrolled thirty or forty of the tenant farmers
under his administration in University of Illinois agricultural
short-courses. One of Lewis Stevenson's close friends and fellow farm-philosophers was George Peek who, in 1933, was
called to Washington by *his* friend Henry Wallace to organ-

ize the Agricultural Adjustment Administration. Adlai Stevenson, like millions of other Americans, had been deeply stirred by Franklin Roosevelt's inaugural address in 1933. Knowing the Depression better than most people, he wanted to do something to help cure it if he could. When Peek asked him to come to Washington to render legal aid to the rapidly expanding AAA, Stevenson responded promptly.

Stevenson's title with the AAA was the high-sounding one of "special counsel." His duties were those of a sort of nation-wide county agent. He toured the country holding hearings and advising regional groups of farmers, ranchers, orchardists and dairymen how to utilize the Act. Then he returned to Washington to try to work out marketing agreements based on reports given him by farmers. As far as history was concerned, Stevenson was unluckier in his associates than Jesse Fell; another member of the AAA's legal division was a spry young ex-secretary to Justice Brandeis named Alger Hiss. By the end of 1933 the AAA was running smoothly and needed Stevenson's services less than the Federal Alcohol Control Administration, set up to handle the legal and tax problems created by the sudden repeal of Prohibition. He served as its assistant general counsel for eight months and then went back to Chicago to rejoin his firm which had now become Sidley, McPherson, Austin and Burgess. There he presently became a partner whose yearly share of the profits soon reached eighteen or twenty thousand dollars.

As a governor of Illinois, and as a presidential possibility, one of Stevenson's principal assets has been his unusual ability as a speaker. When Stevenson talks extemporaneously to small gatherings, he is deft, witty and nimble in reply to questions. When he addresses large audiences on great occasions, his speeches are vigorous in construction, clear in syntax, and eloquent in delivery. Since he had had no platform training and little experience with audiences, professional politicians who backed Stevenson in 1948 wondered where their candidate had acquired his proficiency and supposed he had been born with it. In fact, like Demosthenes, he acquired eloquence by long and diligent practice. Instead of a beach, Stevenson trained on an organization called the Chicago Council on Foreign Relations, of which he was president for one term before he went to Washington and for two more when he returned.

As an inveterate traveler and student of Europe, Stevenson had joined the council soon after his arrival in Chicago, but his election to the presidency posed a problem. Up to that time, his only effort to make himself heard in public had occurred on one of his rare appearances in a courtroom, as counsel in a small case involving an employee of the Wrigley chewing gum company. The judge, a political appointee who perceived a chance to strike a blow for the underdog, asked the nervous Stevenson, "Who did you say retained you, young man?" "P. K. Wrigley," Stevenson quavered. "I don't care if it was John D. Rockefeller and J. P. Morgan," thundered the magistrate. "Don't expect special treatment from this court!"

As president of the council, Stevenson was not called upon to be a Cicero. All he had to do was stand up after a council banquet and introduce the speaker of the evening, in a few well-chosen phrases. The idea that he would do it in a few ill-chosen phrases was what tortured the conscientious Stevenson. The night before his first appearance he wrote out a speech, memorized it carefully, rehearsed it in private and then, lest he forget it, wrote out the first sentence of each paragraph on a little card which he carried in his pocket.

Except that they do not memorize their speeches, most experienced after-dinner orators follow the same system. Stevenson's apparent self-possession and his practiced professional glances at the little card in the palm of his hand convinced his audience that he was a veteran at the game. The speech turned out extremely well and Stevenson followed the same system thereafter, with fewer cards and even more success. Under his leadership, the organization grew as rapidly as the D.A.R. had grown under that of his grandmother. From a miscellaneous clique of trippers and intellectuals, whose intermittent soirees were poorly attended even by these, it became a major civic organization whose bimonthly luncheons regularly attracted a thousand or so of the city's bigwigs.

No less important to the growth of the organization than the president's skill on the platform, which increased with practice, was the state of the world. This had gradually become a matter of grave concern, even to Chicago. As president of the Council on Foreign Relations, Stevenson was placed in the advantageous role of host to visiting European dignitaries whom he had theretofore known only by reputation, as an inconspicuous traveler in the countries they governed. He was also well situated to make advantageous contacts among Chicago's more influential kindred spirits who included Frank Knox, the publisher of the Chicago *Daily News,* and star members of his staff, like Paul Scott Mowrer, who came from Bloomington also. When Roosevelt, building a coalition cabinet to help establish a bipartisan foreign policy, tapped the Republican Knox for Secretary of the Navy in 1940, Knox asked Stevenson to serve under him as soon as he felt he could do more good in Washington than in Chicago, where the reflex reaction to the menace of Adolph Hitler had been the America First Committee.

The day Paris fell, Stevenson became Chicago Chairman of the William Allen White Committee to Defend America by Aiding the Allies. This amounted to a greatly enlarged projection of his job as president of the council. He became a municipal Trojan Horse of Internationalism in the prime citadel of Isolationism. Stevenson brought people like Wendell Willkie, Carl Sandburg and Dorothy Thompson to address mass meetings, one of which, in 1941, filled the Chicago Stadium. Finally, in the summer of that year, he got a phone call from Knox. Says Stevenson: "Knox said, 'Everyone else around Washington has a lawyer and I guess I ought to have one too!' So we packed up and went down there."

Prior to his arrival in Washington, Stevenson had been a close student of history, well situated to scrutinize events like the Depression, the New Deal and the start of World War II. As an actor in it, however, his role — a unique one for a member of his family — was that of supernumerary. On his arrival in Washington, this sorry situation was suddenly and radically altered. Stevenson found himself immediately in the position of the understudy who has to walk on in the star's part, with no time to learn the lines. The way in which this came about constitutes a bit of Rooseveltiana which has somehow thus far slipped through the fine-spun meshes of the war memoirs.

The first job to which Knox assigned Stevenson was preparing legal machinery whereby the Navy, in case it became necessary, could take over the strike-bound Kearney shipyards in New Jersey, then building essential warships. As Stevenson worked on the papers, the strike continued and the need for the ships became more acute. When he finished the plan — which covered rsponsibilities of management, contractual continuances and other legal contingencies — the time for the Navy to utilize it was at hand. The only trouble was that the papers required an executive order signed by the President, who was somewhere off the coast of Newfoundland, returning from the meeting with Churchill at which they had drafted the Atlantic Charter on a battleship. Knox called Stevenson to his office and told him to fly to Quonset, Rhode Island, there get another plane, fly out to meet the cruiser that was bringing the President home, get him to sign the executive order and then fly back to Washington. This would not only save a day in making the papers effective but would also keep the whole affair out of reach of the reporters, who did not know the President's whereabouts.

Stevenson was on the point of departure when Knox called him in a second time. This time Admiral Nimitz was also in the Secretary's office.

"Adlai," said Knox, "the Admiral has a message he wants

you to take to the President and deliver to him in person. Go ahead with the message, Admiral."

"You are to deliver this message to the President and to no one else," said Nimitz. "Tell him that I have learned today, from a heretofore reliable source, that Stalin has opened negotiations with Hitler."

Since this meant, in effect, that Germany had won the war, Stevenson was understandably startled.

"Can I write that down, sir?" he inquired.

"There must be nothing on paper!" said Nimitz, sternly.

"Can I repeat it to you, to make sure I have it right?"

Stevenson recited the message, not once but several times. There was no doubt that he had got it straight. Nimitz and Knox cautioned him again that it was to be delivered to Roosevelt personally, and to Roosevelt alone. No time was to be wasted in doing so. Stevenson then left by plane for Quonset.

At Quonset, he ran into his first difficulties. The weather had closed in. No planes were taking off for anywhere. To find a ship off the Maine coast was out of the question. Stevenson went to the admiral in charge and tried to explain that his mission was of great importance and would brook no interruption. The admiral had seen flurried civilians before, but finally relented somewhat. He said to an aide: "Let this man have a small plane to fly to Rockland, Maine. He might get there by the time the President gets in."

At Rockland, Stevenson's difficulties increased because of the delay at Quonset. From the plane, he could see the President's ship already at the dock and the engine of his special train getting up steam in the station. The pilot landed in a pasture. Stevenson ran from the plane to the highway, hitch-hiked a ride into town with a startled old lady and encountered a six-block traffic jam. Before he could reach the station on foot, the train pulled out. He hitch-hiked back to the airport where the pilot pointed out the train's next stop was Portland, a short distance by air and a long one by rail. Stevenson could at least get there in time to discharge his mission.

At Portland, Stevenson did indeed reach the station well ahead of train time. The trouble now was that another even huger crowd than Rockland's had gathered to meet the President. Maine constables were not impressed by Stevenson's panting assurances that he had a vital message for the chief executive. He was ordered to stand back. Finally, Stevenson elbowed his way through the mob on the platform and caught sight of an acquaintance, Florida's Senator Claude Pepper.

"Well, Adlai, what's the trouble?" asked Pepper. Stevenson told him, not about the Nimitz message but about the Kearney strike papers. Pepper, who himself wanted to board the train to greet the President, was only mildly impressed but said that he would see what could be done. When the train came in, the Senator, who knew the secret service officers, boarded it immediately. Stevenson was relegated to the station platform, where he waited for fifteen minutes, expecting to see the train depart at any second. Finally, Pa Watson appeared at the door of the presidential car. Stevenson explained to Pa that he had some papers for the President.

"Well, can't you give them to me?" asked Roosevelt's

[66]

kindly aide, who had never seen Stevenson before. Stevenson said no. Pa Watson disappeared. Five more minutes slowly passed. Pa Watson reapppeared and told Stevenson the President would see him.

"I got into the car," says Stevenson, "and what do you think I found? There was F.D.R. sitting as relaxed as you please, just as though ten thousand people were not shouting for him on the platform, and just as though he hadn't just settled the world's future with Churchill, and just as though I wasn't bringing the worst news in world history. There were a lot of other people there — Marvin McIntyre, Harry Hopkins, Mrs. Roosevelt and one of the secretaries as well as Pa Watson. They were all having a quiet little bite of supper. F.D.R. looked up when I went in.

" 'Well, Adlai, how are you?' he asked. He had known my father in the first war and I had met him once or twice, years before and very briefly.

"I said I was all right but that I had some papers to show him.

" 'That's fine, Adlai,' he said, 'let's have a look at them.'

"I opened up my brief-case first and got out the Kearney shipyard papers. I showed him the letter of transmittal and all the rest of it, and pointed out where he was supposed to sign. He looked them over for a minute and then said:

" 'Well, yes . . . Now, Adlai you just leave these with me, and I'll read them over. We'll have a meeting at the White House in the morning. You fly back and arrange it. Tell the secretary I'd like to see Myron Taylor and the Attorney General at nine o'clock — and you can be there too.'

" 'But, Mr. President,' I said, 'these are supposed to be signed right now!'

" 'I think it will work out all right this way,' said the President.

" 'Well,' I said, 'if you say so, I guess it will be O.K.' It sounds impossible that even I could talk like such a fool but I was so nervous I hardly knew what I was saying — mostly, I suppose, because I hadn't yet said the really important thing I had on my mind. I could see he was waiting for me to leave, and I had to come out with something. The talk went about like this:

" 'I have something else to tell you, Mr. President.'

" 'Do you, Adlai? What is it?'

" 'Well, Mr. President, it's from Admiral Nimitz. He said to tell you . . . alone.'

" 'Oh, I think you could tell me here, Adlai.'

" 'Can I write it down for you to read?'

" 'Why certainly, Adlai.'

"He gave me a menu and I wrote on the back of it. 'Admiral Nimitz has heard from a heretofore reliable source that Stalin today started negotiations with Hitler.'

Then I gave him back the menu. He read it carefully and then looked up at me.

" 'Adlai,' he said, 'do you believe this?'

"Now that was one thought that had just never crossed my mind. I said: 'Why . . . I don't know, Mr. President.'

" 'I don't believe it,' said F.D.R. " 'I'm not worried at all. Are you worried, Adlai?'

"I said I guessed I wasn't. Then I got up to go. On the way out, in my embarrassed confusion, I walked right into a closed door, thus bending my crooked nose some more. I flew back to Washington, woke Secretary Knox to tell him about the meeting at the White House and we all went over there at nine o'clock. The crowning humiliation to me was that the President hadn't even opened my precious Kearney shipyard papers. He pulled them out and settled the whole business in ten minutes. As for the negotiations between Stalin and Hitler, the President was, of course, right again. Admiral Nimitz's source was unreliable that time. We never heard another word about it."

6

STEVENSON's account of his meeting with Roosevelt in Portland is the kind of story he enjoys telling on himself, embellished with numerous details to show how badly he managed things. While these stories are entertaining, their comic effect often derives from total incongruity with the truth. In the case of the visit to Roosevelt it would have been a sad mistake indeed if Stevenson had honored the idea that a messenger should make haste in accord with his own estimate of the importance of his tidings. As matter of fact, he had handled the assignment admirably; and far from being, as Stevenson now says he suspected at the time, highly amused at his nervous over-eagerness, Roosevelt had been favorably impressed both by the Kearney shipyard papers and by Stevenson's arduous journey, which he heard about from other sources later.

Roosevelt's high opinion of Stevenson was indicated two years later when he gave him the assignment of heading a politico-economic mission to Italy. It was while so engaged that Stevenson came upon an item in the *Stars and Stripes* to which he attributes in large part his later decision to enter politics. "It was a public opinion poll in which seven out of ten American parents said they didn't want their boys to enter public life," says Stevenson. "Think of it! Boys could suffer and die in their cold, muddy, bloody, campaign for the things we believe in but parents didn't want their children to work for those same things. I decided then that if I ever had a chance, I'd go into public life."

Stevenson's handling of the Kearney shipyard situation also had important repercussions. For one thing, the legal machinery devised to apply on that occasion served as the pilot-plan for some sixty other instances in which the government was obliged to take over essential plants in wartime. For another, it got Stevenson into the area of the Navy's labor relations in which, as a liberalizing catalytic agent between the admirals and the unions, he did much to improve them and thus obviate the necessity for even more such seizures. From labor relations, Stevenson progressed to the more intricate problem of the Navy's race relations. As a behind-the-scenes specialist in this field, he helped to modify the tradition whereby Negroes in the Navy had previously served mainly as mess-boys.

In addition to starting Stevenson off on the right foot with the President, the Portland trip set the pace for the rest of his war-time activities. In Washington, Stevenson was given an office next to Knox's from which he fulfilled the role less of an under or assistant secretary than, according to observers at the time, of a sort of alter-ego. Knox was an ebullient, super-energetic executive and one who liked to do things with appropriate fanfare. He was also an ardent exercise devotee who tried to keep up his health by playing golf on the hottest days of the stifling Washington summer. Stevenson was called upon to write Knox's speeches, see swarms of his visitors, especially from outside the service, sit in as his deputy at meetings of the WPB, the BEW, the OWI and numerous other war-born alphabetical agencies, brief him for congressional committee hearings including those of the Truman Committee that investigated war production, talk to the press and otherwise function as an all-around trouble-shooter. Stevenson's duties however were not confined to the capital. On the contrary, he probably covered more ground during the war than anyone else concerned with the possible exceptions of a few DPs, the late Ernie Pyle and Kilroy.

Stevenson's war experiences started in the Navy Department early in the evening of December 7, 1941. His position on that momentous occasion was, as usual, a central one, in Knox's outside office, through which Admiral Stark, the Chief of Naval Operations, and other senior officers passed on their way to give the bad news to the Secretary who was passing it on by telephone to Franklin Roosevelt at the White House. Shortly thereafter his role became less sedentary.

Stevenson's longest excursion into the war zones took place in 1942, in the form of an inspection tour. The area inspected was the entire Pacific theater and the tour involved adventures, even before Knox, Nimitz, Stevenson, aides and other officers had left Pearl Harbor. The plane, a four-motored PB2Y3, no sooner got seventy feet into the air than one engine quit. When the pilot tried to put the plane down again, the sudden torque created by uneven power caused one wing to dip into the water which in turn caused Admiral Nimitz's head to hit the ceiling. With blood matting his silky white hair, the Admiral crawled out the escape hatch and clung to the wing. The other distinguished passengers were less fortunate. The portly Knox, next to attempt escape, got stuck in the hatch and had to be ejected gradually by strenuous prodding from the rear. A crash boat removed the survivors, who included everyone on board, and put them on another PB2Y3. This one smashed a pontoon at Midway. During the party's visit to Canton Island, a Japanese submarine surfaced and fired a few rounds at the local headquarters. This suggested that the tourists had attracted even the attention of the enemy, as did a raid by Jap bombers on the normally peaceful harbor of Espiritu Santo, during their one-night stay there. The group touched at Fiji, Noumea, Palmyra and half a dozen now half-forgotten period place-names before getting back to Washington in February, 1943.

Stevenson's Pacific tour had been preceded by a tour of the Carribean and Canal Zone. It was followed by domestic investigations along both coast lines. These were a warm-up for his major wartime travels in Algeria, Tunis, Sicily, Italy, Gibralter, Liberia, England, France, Germany, Luxembourg, Holland and Belgium. On his first European tour, which started in the summer of 1943, after Mussolini's government had fallen and Italy had joined the Allies, Stevenson headed a Foreign Economic Administration mission which had three objectives. One was to report on how best to keep the Italian economy going and the Italians from starving, while the Allied armies fought their way to the richer industrial North. Another was to report on how to re-establish local government in a nation where all the experienced administrators were presumably Fascists. The third was to report on what elements could be counted to help with these objectives gen-

erally and whether the House of Savoy could be counted on
in particular. The three other members of the mission were
an industrial engineer, an agronomist, and an economist
who spoke Italian. Stevenson had been chosen because it
seemed advisable to have someone in charge who, while not
in one of the services had enough service prestige to command
cooperation in military areas where civilian VIP's sometimes
aroused impatience.

As things developed, Stevenson's experience in VIP mobil-
ity picked up on his previous travels, and his peacetime
familiarity with the terrain and its denizens, proved more
important than his Navy credentials. When he stopped at
the St. George Hotel in Algiers, the Allied GHQ in North
Africa where he had spent part of his honeymoon some years
before, General Eisenhower was too busy to receive him.
The credentials were left with his Chief of Staff, Bedell
Smith, and Stevenson took off for Palermo. His meeting with
the Commander in Chief eventually took place several weeks
later in the corridor of an office building in Naples, where
Eisenhower was conducting an inspection tour. Stevenson
had got across Sicily and up to Naples through the good
offices of the Naval commander at Palermo who, having
identified him as Knox's assistant, thought he might rate a
command car and two blue-jackets.

Eisenhower said, "Well, well, I heard you were here.
How's everything going?"

Stevenson said everything was going as well as could be
expected. He and the General parted on friendly terms, and
have not seen each other since. Stevenson never did retrieve
his papers though he at least got a chance to look for them

two years later when, on his UN assignment in London, he inherited the General's GHQ in Grosvenor Square.

Stevenson's report on Italy, a one-hundred and twenty-two page secret document, covering agriculture, industry, communications, currency, transportation and import problems, was generally regarded in Washington as a model of its type. It served first as the basis for high-level policy decisions in Italy, and later for analogous ones in the case of Germany. When he finished collecting material for this Stevenson made plans to go home. The journey included a stop in Dakar where he ran into his old friend, Admiral William Glassford.

In Italy, Stevenson had seen a lot of Carlo Sforza, the Italian statesman, whom he had encountered previously in the Council on Foreign Relations. Glassford suggested that on the way back to Washington, Stevenson drop in at Liberia, which was being considered as the possible site of a post-war port and submarine base, if its harbor facilities proved adaptable to the purpose. This struck an echo from the even more distant past, since Liberia was where Stevenson's great grandfather and fellow-Princetonian, Dr. Lewis Ward Green, had sent his slaves when he freed them a century or so before. Stevenson agreed to go, taking along an old friend named Wesley Sturges whom he had known in his AAA era and who later became Dean of the Yale Law School. From Liberia, Stevenson went back to Washington to furnish Knox with a postscript on that part of the world and catch his breath before starting off somewhere else.

As things turned out, he had no chance to catch his breath before Knox died, on April 29, 1944, of heart failure brought on by overwork and exercise. Knox's successor, James Forrestal, was a close friend of Stevenson's with whom he had sometimes sneaked in a set or two of tennis along with Admiral Jerry Land and whoever they could get for a fourth, on summer afternoons. However, on the assumption that the new Secretary would want to appoint his own assistants, Stevenson resigned and returned to Chicago to help a group of Chicago *News* employees buy the paper from the Knox estate with the aid of outside capital which they asked Stevenson to round up for them.

Stevenson found the capital but his bid was turned down in favor of a higher one and a month or so later he found himself on an Army Air Force mission to evaluate strategic bombing damage in Germany, for guidance in the forthcoming occupation and the subsequent bombing of Japan. This got him to Spa in time for a meeting with General Patton that was cut short when General Bradley paid an unexpected call to discuss a secret matter. The secret matter was the Battle of the Bulge out of which Stevenson, unaware that it was going on, drove to Brussels and flew back to England in a fog so dense that a guide with a lantern had to walk in front of the car that took them from the airport, at which they had made an emergency landing, to the station to catch a train for London. From London, then reverberating from V-2 blasts, Stevenson flew back to Libertyville, in time for Christmas.

Stevenson's second visit to Europe concluded his active contributions to the waging of World War II. His contributions toward stopping it, which began shortly afterwards, were less undramatic. They started with a phone call from Archibald MacLeish inviting him to take on a trouble-shooting chore for the State Department. The chore was to help promote public understanding of the forthcoming United Nations Conference at San Francisco, scheduled for April, 1945. Stevenson demurred at first but finally proceeded to Washington in time to collaborate with MacLeish on the proclamation announcing the death of President Roosevelt on April 12th. Stevenson did the research for this document, in the form of looking up what had been said on previous occasions when chief executives had died in office. MacLeish attended to composing it, for issuance the next day.

Whether Roosevelt's death, at precisely the high water mark of Allied fortunes, was a final instance of that sense of advantageous timing of which he was a noted master, or whether his departure from the scene caused some of the trouble that soon followed it, is a question for historians to settle. In any case, no sooner had he been laid to rest than the nations that had fought a common foe in comparative compatability began to bicker with each other. The bickering began as soon as they all sat down to talk about peace and, so far as the U. S. delegation was concerned, included internal as well as external disagreements.

The U. S. delegation to San Francisco included Senators Connally and Vandenberg, Congressmen Eaton and Bloom, Harold Stassen, John Foster Dulles, Secretary of State Edward Stettinius and a large staff of experts on the topics likely to appear on the agenda. As Secretary of State and Chairman of the U. S. delegation and the Conference,

Stettinius had a hard row to hoe. He was just past forty and the other members, including even Stassen, were not only his senior in years but mostly men, at least in their own opinion, of presidential stature. The leadership of the Secretary proved to be, according to some irritable observers, scarcely more inspired than his choice for the job had been in the first place and he was soon being referred to disrespectfully as "Junior."

Junior's difficulties were not confined to his delegation. The whole population of the U. S., as represented in San Francisco by correspondents from every paper from the New York *Times* to the Plumbers' *Gazette,* were upset because they could not find anyone who knew what was going on or, if he knew, was telling. Unable to get news from their own delegates, the correspondents had eventually descended to getting it from others, including Russians. Indignant editorials about this state of things appeared in various papers, including the Washington *Post.* The *Post's* publisher, Eugene Myers, and Junior were living on the same floor of the Fairmount Hotel. When they met in the corridor, waiting for an elevator, they came to blows before the car arrived. To correct these sad conditions, Arthur Krock, the correspondent of the New York *Times,* offered a sage suggestion. He said: "Send for Adlai."

When Stevenson arrived early in May, his first move was to arrange to attend the U. S. delegation's meetings so that he would be aware of what was going on inside them. His next move was to establish himself, after the meetings, in Room 576 at the Fairmount, whence he dispensed information to the correspondents. The correspondents were so thirsty for news, and Stevenson provided such a lot of it, that Room

576 was crowded day and night. Stevenson's job became known as Operation Titanic, and so much news leaked out that U. S. delegation members now began to complain that they could not talk to themselves without seeing their thoughts in the headlines. Nonetheless, their pique with Stevenson was greatly outweighed by satisfaction in their improved notices. Before anyone got around to plugging Operation Titanic, the conference was over and the delegations getting ready for the Preparatory Commission meeting in London, scheduled for the following August.

Stevenson's job at the London meeting was that of deputy to Stettinius, who having resigned as Secretary of State after the San Francisco Conference, headed the U. S. delegation with the rank of ambassador. When he arrived in London after a pleasant crossing accompanied by the new Secretary of State James Byrnes, Charles Bohlen, Ben Cohen, Foster Dulles and other State Department notables en route to the conference of Foreign Ministers, Stevenson found Stettinius more in need of medical than diplomatic advice. His gall bladder was troubling him, among other things, and he presently returned to the U. S. to have it removed, leaving Stevenson in charge.

Stevenson's confreres at the commission meeting were diplomats of wide repute like Philip Noel-Baker and Gladwyn Jebb of England, René Massigli of France, and the urbane Wellington Koo of China. Since even the representatives of places like Bolivia or Syria had ambassadorial rank, Stevenson, as the representative of the most powerful nation of all, and the one that had instigated the whole affair, was somewhat handicapped by being only a minister. Instead of the suite at Claridge's from which Stettinius had operated, he and his wife and their two older sons, who went to Harrow as day scholars, lived in a small converted bomb-damaged stable, staffed by one elderly female cook.

Possibly the knottiest problem confronting the Preparatory Commission was that of a permanent site for the U. N. This involved much wrangling, good natured and otherwise, among the delegates who found themselves besieged by boosters from places which considered themselves pre-eminently qualified, from Boston to the Black Hills of South Dakota. San Francisco, a leading contender for the honor, sent a handsome brochure outlining its advantages which included a picture of a line of can-can girls. Gromyko, when he saw the brochure, which had been left open at this page for his inspection, raised his eyebrows.

"Gentlemen," he announced to a group that had gathered to discuss the subject, "this I did not see in San Francisco."

While the Foreign Ministers' conference bogged down in one impasse after another, the meeting of the Preparatory Commission proceeded, in an atmosphere of comparative harmony, to cover considerable ground. Its chief impediment proved to be the Soviet assumption that the world was divided into three areas: the U. S. S. R. and its satellites, the British Empire including Western Europe and the U. S., including Central and South America. Meanwhile, the aplomb developed by Stevenson at Foreign Relations Council banquets came in handy at the round of diplomatic dinners and receptions with which the delegates supplemented meager British rations and celebrated their professional reunion.

When the Preparatory Commission adjourned in December, Stevenson had three weeks in which to prepare for the arrival of the U. S. delegation to the first meeting of the General Assembly, composed of Messrs. Stettinius, Byrnes, Dulles, Vandenberg, Eaton and Bloom, Mrs. Roosevelt, and a score or so of foreign service officers and experts including Alger Hiss, with whom Stevenson had renewed his AAA acquaintance previously in San Francisco and Washington. As "senior advisor" to a delegation that stood in need of lots of advice about almost everything. Stevenson had his hands full again. Having achieved its main purpose of adopting the structure proposed by the Commission, selecting a secretary general and deciding who was to be what on which of its innumerable committees, the assembly adjourned in February.

Stevenson's varied and protracted efforts to get the United Nations organization under way, though largely unpublicized, were undoubtedly one of the few effective accomplishments of U. S. diplomacy since the war. Back in the U. S., Stevenson was offered State Department posts including an under secretaryship and embassies in Brazil or Argentina, neither of which he had money enough to support. He returned to law practice in Chicago until Truman appointed him an alternate delegate to the second session of the General Assembly in New York. When that session ended in November, Stevenson went back to Chicago again, and practiced law till the next session, in the autumn of 1947.

As the 1947 autumn meeting of the General Assembly drew to a close, Stevenson felt constrained to decide once and for all whether he was going to rejoin his law firm in Chicago, on which he had been paying what amounted to courtesy calls for six years, or whether to strike out into something new. His mind went back to the report of the public opinion poll he had seen in Italy, but, if he was to enter public life, another question arose immediately. This was: how to do it?

7

In considering a career in politics, Stevenson was behaving in a characteristically conscientious fashion. His considerations, however, had one serious drawback. They were unilateral. Going into U. S. politics entails getting elected to something. Getting elected entails the help of practicing politicians.

Stevenson's qualifications for getting elected to almost anything were valid, not to say sensational. Moreover his record, in the form of distinguished service all over the world, throughout the greatest crisis in world history, not to mention the similar previous records compiled by a quorum of his forebears, were written so that all who ran might read. The only trouble was that politicians rarely run; and they almost never read anything except the election returns. Thus, so far as Stevenson's record was concerned, it counted for nothing. The politicians had never heard of Stevenson.

Possibly the most astute and authoritative Democratic politician on the Chicago postwar scene was the Chairman of the Cook County Democratic Committee, a small shrewd man named Colonel Jacob M. Arvey. Arvey, the son of immigrants, had grown up in the Loop district, worked as an errand boy, studied for his law degree in night school, rounded up votes for district leaders, and been elected to the

City Council in 1923. The feat that put him on the political map occurred during the bitter gubernatorial campaign of 1936, when his ward delivered 29,000 votes to 700 for the opposition. Prior to World War II, Arvey had been considered a champion at in-fighting in a city noted for pulling no punches in the precincts. During the war, in which he had volunteered and served in New Guinea, two things had happened to Arvey. One was that his investments at home had prospered enough to make financial incentives less compelling than they had been previously. The other was that like Stevenson, he had apparently done some idealistic brooding and had reached the conclusion that the nation needed and deserved some honest public servants. Arvey was, however, better situated than Stevenson to supply the deficiency.

The important thing about Arvey's discovery of Stevenson was not that it came considerably later than the discovery of Stevenson by disinterested persons in relatively remote parts of the world like Washington, D. C., San Francisco, London and Liberia. It was that, in making it, the Colonel was far ahead of all his Chicago colleagues. The discovery took place at a luncheon given by Senate Secretary Lester Biffle late in July of 1947. Arvey was taken to this luncheon by Illinois' Senator Scott Lucas, whom he had come to consult about naming a U. S. Attorney for the Northern District of Illinois, a job that requires senatorial confirmation. In addition to Biffle, Lucas, and Arvey, Senator Tom Connally, Secretary Byrnes and one or two others of comparable national stature were present at the table. The conversation was general. When Byrnes heard talk about some sort of

Illinois appointment out of the corner of his ear, he dropped what he was saying and turned to Arvey:

"Don't you people in Illinois know you've got a gold nugget out there?" he inquired.

"Who do you mean?" asked Arvey.

"I mean Adlai Stevenson!" said Byrnes.

"Adlai Stevenson? Who's he?" inquired Arvey.

Byrnes and some of the others present then proceeded to enlighten him.

In seeking this enlightenment, Arvey was not entirely disingenuous. The fact was that he had already made up his mind about his candidate for the U. S. Attorney's office. It was Otto Korner Jr., who was afterwards appointed to it. What Arvey was looking for were bigger fish: candidates to run for governor and senator in the next year's election.

When Arvey got back to Chicago, he began tactfully to investigate the rumor he had heard about the nugget. First, he telephoned his good friend Judge Harry M. Fisher who was, it turned out, a Stevenson admirer. Fisher said among other things that Stevenson was "a great liberal" and suggested that further data might be forthcoming from Mrs. Eleanor Roosevelt, of whom Arvey was an admirer. In due course a luncheon was arranged by Fisher at which Arvey and Stevenson met for the first time. Arvey casually asked Stevenson his views on labor, civil rights, economy and other controversial state and national issues. Stevenson's replies impressed him. So did another incident that occurred a few days later.

Stevenson and Arvey were not the only Americans who had time to do a little serious thinking during the war. Another such was Louis Kohn, a young Chicago attorney, who had also served in New Guinea where he sometimes encountered Arvey. "I used to wonder how I had come to get there," says Kohn. "I figured that it was the fault of every American who had neglected to take an interest in getting good government at home. I had neglected it as much as anyone but, right there, I changed." Kohn's new interest in international affairs lead him to attend a meeting of the Council on Foreign Relations at which Stevenson, himself just back from England, was the speaker. After the meeting, Kohn pursued Stevenson to his office, where he urged him to enter politics.

Stevenson displayed enough interest to cause Kohn to carry the matter further. He went to two influential Chicagoans who were admirers of Stevenson. One was his close friend and Lake Forest neighbor, Hermon Dunlap Smith, an insurance executive with whom he now quite often spends weekends. The other was Stephen Mitchell, an Irish Catholic lawyer who knew Stevenson less well but politics better. The upshot of Kohn's activities was that he, Smith and Mitchell formed a "Stevenson for Senator Committee." When they had two dozen or so influential names signed up, they paid a call on Kohn's New Guinea crony, Colonel Arvey.

By the time he saw Kohn, Smith and Mitchell, Arvey was partly sold on the idea of proposing Stevenson to his Cook County Committee for one of the top spots on the ticket. After further meetings with Stevenson which included a weekend at Lake Forest with the Smiths, he became entirely sold. Recommendation by Arvey was tantamount to a nomination. Now, however, uncertainty developed about which spot it should be. While he had been investigating Stevenson, Arvey had also been investigating another promising politico named Paul Douglas.

Douglas was a University of Chicago Economics professor who had enlisted in the Marines as an over-age private, worked his way up to a commission, and seen combat, among other spots, at Okinawa. The incumbent Republican senator was an older ex-marine named Curley Brooks whose campaign tactics had always included copious references to his feats on the battlefields of World War I and his possession of the Croix de Guerre. Arvey thought Douglas could deal with Brooks effectively on a marine to marine basis. Furthermore, Douglas was an impassioned orator and a socio-economic theorist of considerable persuasive powers. These qualifications, while they would show to advantage in a legislative body, were qualities which might be wasted in an administrative post, for which his aptitudes were debatable anyway. Arvey therefore proposed to run Douglas for the Senate and Stevenson for governor.

From Stevenson's point of view, this proposal at first seemed preposterous. His thoughts about entering politics had been based on the notion that, as a longtime student and seasoned practitioner in the field of foreign policy, he might be of some use in the Senate. However, while the governorship had not crossed his mind, he did not want to impede Douglas, an old friend whose enlistment he had helped to facilitate as assistant to the Secretary of the Navy. The resultant indecision upon Stevenson's part set a record which was not exceeded by him until he was faced with an even bigger choice last spring. With a matter of hours to go

before the December 31st, 1947 deadline, the decision he
finally reached on this occasion was affirmative.

In putting Stevenson across with other party leaders, Arvey
had certain obvious disadvantages of which the most conspicuous was a corollary of the one that he himself had
recently overcome. This was that none of them knew Stevenson, and that they all knew that few of the voters knew him.
When they looked Stevenson over, their doubts were not
as readily resolved as Arvey's had been, because they lacked
Arvey's influential contacts. The horrible rumor about Oxford was only one of many that the Colonel was obliged to
deal with. Delegations of ward heelers came to complain to
him. The burden of their woes was summed up by the
spokesman for a Northside precinct.

"Where the hell did you dig up this guy Add-lay?" he
inquired sadly. "Let alone not knowing him, the voters
can't even pronounce his name. He'll get his ears beat back."

Balanced against Stevenson's liabilities were certain un-
deniable assets. Among these, the least impressive was his
record in Washington, Europe and the UN. Neither the
Navy nor the rights of minorities in Iran count for much
with the voters of Illinois. Somewhat more important was
his family background, which suggested that even if only
his relatives voted for him, he would pile up a fairly substantial total. The most important argument of all, in persuading
the ward heelers to accept him, was that no one really
expected him to win.

In the winter of 1948, even Democrats thought it was sure

to be a Republican year. A Chicago Republican leader told Dewey that Stevenson had no more chance of winning in Illinois than he had of spitting up Niagara Falls. Dewey later informed Stevenson that his sole satisfaction in the 1948 election was that it enabled him to ask his misguided informant to perform this interesting experiment. Democrats were only a little more optimistic. The idea was to run someone who, even in losing, would confer respectability upon the ticket.

In view of the probabilities in the election for one thing, and of the difficulties in overcoming Stevenson's scruples about running for governor for another, some points that are usually inspected carefully beforehand had been wholly overlooked. One of these came to light when Stevenson, Arvey and their publicity campaign manager, Spike Hennessey, were riding to Springfield to accept his nomination from the State Committee.

"By the way, Jack," asked Stevenson. "Do you think I ought to make a political speech to these fellows? You know, I've never really made one."

It was explained to the candidate that, on the occasion of accepting a gubernatorial nomination, a speech was usually in order.

"Well, what do you think I ought to say to them?" inquired Stevenson.

Arvey explained that, as the candidate, it was Stevenson's privilege to say anything he wanted. "Maybe you should think what you would do if you were governor and just tell them that," he suggested.

"Well, I do have some ideas, of course." said Stevenson.

"I suppose I'll make a mess of it, as usual, but still, I'll go back to the club-car and try to work out something."

"He went back to the club-car for an hour," says Arvey, recalling the incident. "When he came back, he had a speech that would take about eight minutes to deliver. Hennessey and I read over it and then looked at each other.

" 'Don't ever let anyone change a word of it, or of any speech you ever write,' was what I said to him," says Arvey. "You've got a new approach to politics entirely."

Stevenson's new approach — a down-to-earth one in which he said what he meant in as few words as possible, seasoned with wit, common sense and conviction — pleased voters as much as it pleased Mr. Arvey. Nonetheless, as the campaign progressed, even this approach seemed hardly an adequate weapon with which to win the election and few others were available. Many of Stevenson's friends, Republicans as well as Democrats, had often urged him to enter politics and promised to provide financial support if and when he did so. Approached in the autumn of 1948, most of them seemed to feel that the time was singularly inopportune. Stevenson's campaign managers rarely had more than a few hundred dollars in their treasury. Once, when they desperately needed $200 to pay for a radio program, Hermon Smith was on his way to get credit or cancel it when he saw an old friend on the corner and button-holed him for a loan. Finally, on top of the money shortage, the candidate seemed somewhat slow to catch on to standard political techniques.

In conducting a political campaign, the standard technique is for the candidate to promise as many potential supporters as many things as possible, in the effort to secure votes. This makes things difficult for him when he gets into office but, since it is presumed to be impossible to get into office otherwise, the method is almost universally practiced.

Stevenson chose a different one. He promised nobody anything, including Colonel Arvey. On the contrary, before consenting to run at all, he made Arvey promise him something.

Explaining that he thought himself better qualified for the Senate than for the Executive Mansion, he said to Arvey: "I'm not a politician. I'll do a lot of things the organization wouldn't stand for. I won't make political appointments. I'll get you into a lot of trouble."

Arvey felt constrained to assure Stevenson that he would have a free hand with appointments and need only appoint Democrats if he was sure they qualified.

Not long afterward, Arvey was with Stevenson when two important labor leaders came to pay a call at his headquarters.

"We are here to support you," said one of the leaders, "but we don't want any misunderstandings. We want you to appoint a member of our union as labor director. And we'd like Jack, here, to be a witness, when you say you'll do it."

"Stevenson," says Arvey, "looked that fellow in the eye and said something that took courage. He said: 'I need you men and I need your support. But I haven't made any promises and I'm not making any. I may pick a man from your union. Then again, I may not. Jack Arvey here, hasn't asked me for any commitments. If he doesn't, why should you?' I knew right then that he was no striped-pants diplomat."

Stevenson's campaign was based on the issue of corruption, as exemplified in the regime of the incumbent Dwight Green, who opposed him. Corruption in Illinois state politics is an old, old story. The estimable Henry Horner had done a fine job in his first term but in the course of it, marked coolness developed between him and the redoubtable Edward Kelly of the famous Kelly-Nash duumvirate. In the campaign of 1936, Kelly had set out to smash Horner. Horner only won by squeezing votes out of every state office holder and making commitments to anyone who had votes to offer.

Partly because of such commitments, Horner's second term, during which his health deteriorated rapidly, was less successful than his first. No real scandal developed however, until after his death, which took place three months before the term expired. There then began the "hundred days" of Illinois politics, somewhat less glorious ones than Napoleon's, during which Horner's political heirs hastened to take advantage of their unexpected opportunity. Working, as it were, on golden time, the new regime scrawled such a sorry record that not even the many thousands of gallons of white paint bought from a paint contractor friend of the lieutenant governor sufficed wholly to conceal it. It was in protest against the graft of this regime that that of Green had been elected. Green had been an assistant U. S. Attorney at the time of Al Capone's conviction for tax evasion and was widely credited for convicting him. No one doubted that there had been some conniving during the Green regime but Green

Lewis Green Stevenson with daughter Elizabeth and son Adlai Ewing in 1902 at Charlevoix, Michigan, where the family spent most summer vacations.

Home of Adlai E. Stevenson I in Bloomington, Illinois, had wide porch, rose trellis and captain's walk.

Sailing was a favorite summer sport at Charlevoix, an old-fashioned, informal resort on Lake Michigan.

Adlai E. Stevenson, at three, poses at Charlevoix with his sister Elizabeth
("Buffie"), who is now Mrs. Ernest L. Ives.

Kite flying at age of four, Adlai Stevenson is encouraged by his sister, standing at extreme right. Adlai's family nickname was "Laddie."

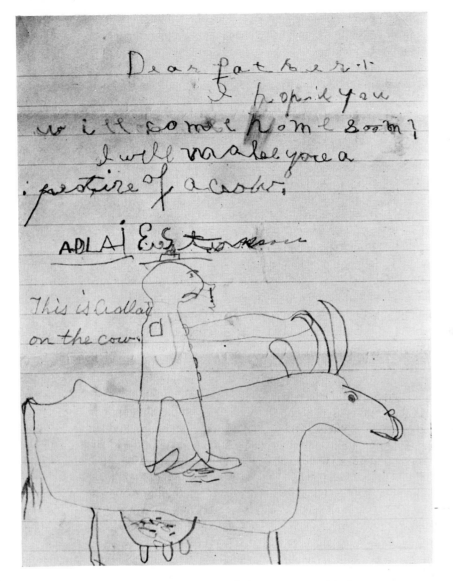

First recorded literary composition of Governor was this letter to his father written when he was seven. Animal seems to show Thurber influence.

Tennis was Stevenson's best sport at Choate School, where he was too light for football. Governor still plays fair game.

At Lausanne, Switzerland in 1912, Stevenson family went sightseeing in old-fashioned Packard touring car.

At thirteen, Adlai Stevenson wore
Eton collar.

At fifteen, he attended high school
at Normal, Illinois.

At twenty-six, Adlai passed bar
exams at Northwestern.

Growing bald in 1951, Governor
still looks youthful.

Mrs. Stevenson with sons Adlai III and Borden. Governor's former wife lives in Chicago, writes expert light verse, has lately helped manage *Poetry* magazine.

Mrs. Borden Stevenson, who divorced the Governor in 1949, with their eldest son, Adlai III.

was well liked; and, after all, it was a Republican year.

Halfway through the Illinois campaign of 1948, a gambler was murdered in Peoria. The St. Louis *Post-Dispatch,* an out-of-state paper with a big circulation in southern Illinois, sent a reporter to dig into the causes. The reporter found evidences of an alliance between gamblers and law enforcement officers. The Green administration rashly tried to discredit both the exposé and the reporter. The *Post-Dispatch,* joined by the Chicago Daily *News,* got down to business and dug further. What they uncovered proved to be exceptional even for Illinois.

It developed that numerous officials in the Green administration had been steadily engaged in shaking down gamblers, slot machine operators and punchboard distributors. Government payrolls were loaded with useless and in some cases non-existent employees. Property was bought at wildly inflated prices from friends of the administration. Cheating and kicking back on state contracts was standard practice. Scores of newspaper editors who might be deemed to know about such matters, and potentially capable of writing about them, were carried on the state payrolls for thousands of dollars a month. Since this was just about the sort of thing that Stevenson had been charging, its appearance in cold print from an objective source provided his campaign with fresh momentum.

Green's campaign against Stevenson had been lethargic, patterned on the national one, on whose success it was expecting to carry the state. About the worst things that Green had found to say about Stevenson was that he was a "cookie-pusher" and a "striped-pants diplomat." When some of Stevenson's old cronies on the Chicago *News* reported that its files contained no pictures of Stevenson in striped pants, and printed one of Green wearing not only striped pants, but a top hat, cutaway and white waistcoat as well, this aspersion lost its cogency.

Early in October a friend spied Stevenson on a streetcar, going from his office to the station. Two months before, the friend would have felt inclined to jump off the car again, to avoid being touched for a campaign contribution. Changed circumstances emboldened him to ask how the campaign was going.

"It's going too well," said Stevenson. "I think I'm going to get elected."

When Stevenson defeated Green by 572,000 votes, while Truman was nosing out Dewey in Illinois by a mere 34,000, or more than half a million less, it was one of the most dramatic reversals of the they-laughed-when-I-sat-down-at-the-piano variety ever recorded in the long history of U. S. politics. However, the politicians seemed to feel that the joke, somehow or other, was still on Stevenson. Immediately after election, in thanking a large group of ward leaders for their efforts during the campaign, the Governor-elect added that his only regret was that he would have to leave so many loyal friends behind when he moved to Springfield.

"Don't you worry, Adlai," shouted someone in the crowd, "we will all be there."

The ward leaders were there, to be sure, but it did them very little good. The selection of Stevenson as a tyro candidate for provincial office long after the rest of the world knew him as a master of diplomatic maneuvering was one of the ironies of the 1948 campaign. The election to office of a candidate deemed wholly unelectable — as amazing as a butchering of the executioner by the sacrificial lamb — had been another. The final irony, however, remained to be revealed.

In accepting Stevenson as a nominee for governor, Chicago's seasoned professional politicians had been operating on the entirely plausible theory that if, by any amazing chance, he were to get elected, he could immediately be taught to play ball and that, if he proved inept, he could be readily dropped from the roster at the next election. The discoveries first that Stevenson had no intention of playing ball and, second, that far from being expendable he was the state's greatest political asset in a century was only made by them later on, and then with by no means unmixed delight.

8

THE QUALITY of surprise engendered, among politicians generally, and Illinois politicians in particular, by Stevenson's performance as Governor of Illinois springs from a little understood fact about the virtue of honesty. In the abstract, honesty is the same everywhere. In practice, it differs qualitatively in different callings, owing to the influence in each of its special *esprit de corps*. Thus, without being accused of dishonesty, theatrical people proverbially give priority over all else to creating an illusion, i.e., deceiving the public, in what is recognized as a harmless manner. Lawyers may plead innocence for guilty clients without betraying their professional code. Wicked brokers may bilk their customers but a nod is good as gold on the stock exchange. Even honor among thieves, as gangster murders to punish infringements of it amply testify, is by no means an empty phrase. Politics, too, has its special kind of honesty. In this kind of honesty, loyalty to other politicians, repayment of political favors in kind or cash and absolute fidelity to pledges often not only unwritten but unspoken have priority over loyalty to the public interest.

It is not hard to see why this should be so. Politicians make a living out of politics and sympathize with each other's difficulties in doing so. However, while the special brands of honesty exemplified in most other callings are not usually a matter of wide general interest, and thus often pass without disparaging comment, the special brand of honesty exemplified in politics is, by definition, a matter of public concern; and the public, moreover, naively expects politicians to give priority to its interests rather than to each other's. This results in frequent misunderstandings between the public and its public servants. It creates what might be called the public servant problem in which, when the public angrily complains of being imposed upon, the public servants respond with sincere feelings of injured innocence.

Never having been in politics before, Stevenson was unencumbered by the political obligations normally incurred by any politician long before he reaches such eminence as a governorship. In addition to this, and what was even more important, he was hardly aware that such obligations existed, let alone of the importance that attached to them among his new associates. He brought to politics only honesty of the lay variety, and acted as though that were the only kind. Politicians were horrified not so much by his reformer's zeal as by his failure to observe their code which they put down to his perhaps pardonable ignorance. A classic example of this apparent ignorance on Stevenson's part cropped up immediately, in the form of his introduction into the legislature of a bill to reform the state police force.

The Illinois state police force consists of five hundred uniformed constables whose salaries are around $400 each per month. Their far from onerous duties traditionally consisted of acting as chauffeurs and performing political chores for state officials. The qualifications for this type of public

service were not elevated ones. Prior to Stevenson's in-
cumbency, the convention had been for each new administration to dismiss all the state policemen appointed by the
opposition party and install new ones of its own. By the time
Stevenson had been sworn in, his dutiful party leaders,
mindful of the precepts of political honesty, had lists of party
workers, and party workers' friends and relatives, who seemed
eligible as replacements for the Republican police force.

For Stevenson to have preserved the system of appointing
state policemen on a patronage basis would have been quite
in line not only with state tradition but also with family
tradition as founded by the Headsman. Instead, his grandson
calmly announced that he planned to put the state police
department to work, in a law enforcement capacity. Further,
he announced that its personnel would be chosen on the
merit system, i.e., after examination of applicants as to their
qualifications for their new and unaccustomed duties. Finally,
he had a bill introduced into the legislature, to enact this
plan into law.

The howl that went up from Democratic politicians at
this was similar in tone to that of a small child punished
when it is not aware of being naughty. "He's ruining the
Democratic party," screamed one ward leader to Colonel
Arvey. "A sneaky trick," protested another one. Even Arvey,
who had been aware of the Governor's intention, was awed
by his method of effecting it. "I thought he would offer them
something in return," says Arvey, " some sort of compromise
or other. But the Governor offered nothing. Of course, in
the long run, he was right. Good government gets more votes

than handing out jobs, but it is hard to make a precinct captain see it that way."

In fact, since the police merit system bill was so amended in the legislature as to guarantee political equality on the force, it worked no long-term injury on Stevenson's own party. The force was almost exclusively composed of Republican appointees, at the time of his election. The bill, as passed, called for the division of the 500-man force equally between Democrats and Republicans. Thereafter, replacements would be made on the merit plan. With generous Republican backing as well as the support of reluctantly obedient Democrats, the bill swept through both houses and set the tone for the rest of Stevenson's first administration.

When Stevenson took office in 1948, he inherited a state in which: Three thousand miles of highway were in urgent need of immediate repair or reconstruction; mental hospitals were overcrowded, obsolete and understaffed; aid to public schools were less per capita than in any other state in the union; illicit gambling operated with the professional endorsement of local police; payrolls were padded but legitimate state salaries had not been raised to meet the cost of living; charges of every sort of corruption, often well-founded, had undermined confidence in the government generally; and an eighty-year-old state constitution so framed as to be practically amendment-or revision-proof, made it difficult if not impossible to get at the source of many of these and other deficiencies.

In three and a half years in office, Stevenson effected some noteworthy changes.

Roads. During the early nineteen twenties the somewhat Roman proclivities of the late Governor Len Small included road-building which, as the biggest single item in state expenditures legitimate and otherwise, are the biggest and most obvious item on any list of gubernatorial responsibilities. Whether or not the Small regime profited unduly by doing so, it at least provided Illinois with one of the first and best state highway systems. The Small road system, however, had not been designed to withstand the ravages of heavy-duty trucking. This, the shortage of maintenance crews during the war and mere old age had caused the entire Illinois road system to start crumbling more or less simultaneously in 1948. Stevenson set his newly reformed state police force to policing overweight trucks, instead of cheerfully waving them on their way. He raised truck registration fees and gas taxes to provide new revenue. Lastly, he reorganized the highway division, to eliminate graft in handling contracts and get set for a major building program. The program, a ten-year one, calling for the eventual expenditure of some $100,000,000, is now under way, and will result in a complete renovation and modernization of the entire 12,000-mile highway system.

Schools. In 1948, Illinois' per capita rate of state aid to local schools was among the lowest in the U. S. Stevenson immediately advocated spending an additional $112,000,000 and proposed broadening the base of the state sales tax to provide the funds for this and some other similar forms of local aid. When the sales tax bill was defeated, aid to the schools had to be cut back 10 percent but nonetheless during his term the state's contribution to schools rose by $139,000,000. Illinois' educational program is now generally regarded as one of the nation's best.

Mental Hospitals, like roads, are purely a state responsibility. Illinois' twenty eight hospitals, housing 47,000 patients, in 1948 closely resembled enlarged Bedlams, partly because their 3,500 attendants were all political appointees. Stevenson called the heads of the hospitals into conference to find out what they really needed. He appointed Fred Hoehler, an internationally known expert in rehabilitation, to head the Welfare Department. Under Hoehler, 85 percent of the attendants were put under civil service. Thousands of patients capable of being cared for at home were dislodged from the overcrowded hospitals. Thousands of others capable of paying their own way in whole or in part were required to do so. By 1950, Dr. Karl Menninger of the famous Kansas Clinic, was invited to inspect the hospitals to see what improvements had been made and what further ones were needed. Menninger pronounced the Illinois Mental Hospitals among the best in the country.

Personnel. Illinois has had civil service provisions covering most state jobs since 1905. However, the civil service law specifies that, when a certified appointee is not available, a non-certified one may be temporarily appointed instead. Politicians dislike certified employees because, being almost immune to firing, they make less enthusiastic party workers than employees who have the sword of dismissal over their heads. Furthermore, this preference can be plausibly rationalized on the ground that the lack of incentive makes civil service workers indolent in their real jobs. While not alto-

ADLAI E. STEVENSON

gether sold on civil service, Stevenson considers it superior
to patronage. He encouraged civil service inspectors boards
to examine appointees in as many branches of the state
employment as possible. This was an arduous and unspec-
tacular process but the results have been notable. Thousands
of jobs which were previously filled by "temporary," i.e.,
political, appointees are now filled by certified civil service
employees. Especially important is the increased ratio of civil
service employees in the state's corps of field investigators,
who previously had been especially in demand as political
field workers.

Economy. In the course of bringing the state budget into
balance, Stevenson contrived not only to increase expenditures on roads and schools but also to raise legitimate state
salaries 10 percent, most of the difference being squeezed out
of existing revenues by firing 1,300 superfluous employees,
holding new construction to a minimum and paring down
politically advantageous contributions from state funds to
local pressure groups. Illinois currently ranks lower in per
capita tax collection in relation to per capita income than
any other states except Nebraska and New Jersey. Unlike
almost every other state, it has not raised general revenue
taxes since 1948. While the average of other states total appropriations were rising 22 percent, Illinois appropriations
rose only 12 percent. The consensus of opinion appears to be
that Stevenson's economies have been effected not at the
expense of needed services but by means of more efficient
administration and more careful expenditure.

Administrative Methods. Stevenson put through seventy-
eight bills aimed at technical improvements on the efficiency

of governmental machinery. He reorganized the State Commerce Commission, which sets utility rates, on a bipartisan basis. He tried to get a fair employment practice bill and failed by only one vote. And he survived two potentially disastrous scandals.

One of the scandals was the discovery that state meat inspectors were being bribed to pass horse meat for beef for use in hamburgers. The other was the discovery of the practice of counterfeiting cigarette stamps. The usual procedure in such cases is to get the attorney general to investigate and pin the blame on someone outside the regime. Stevenson lead both exposés himself and employed lie-detector tests on his own inspectors.

To professional politicians, not the least astonishing feature of the Stevenson regime has been the Governor's success in enlisting the cooperation of his own party's disconcerted bosses and especially that of the senate's Democratic minority leader, a battle-scarred veteran of the Chicago precinct wars named Bill Connors. Instead of becoming impatient with Stevenson's innovations. Connors developed a protective feeling for him. Connors calls Stevenson "the little fellow in the mansion," and nurses his pet projects through the mills of legislation like a Damon Runyon gambler caring for a foundling.

Underlying many of the other ills of Illinois state government when Stevenson took office was the constitution itself. This eighty-year-old instrument had become sadly outdated in many respects but in three in particular. One was the tax provision whereby, since no distinction was made between real estate and other personal property, taxes fell chiefly on land, thus preventing effective revision of the state's whole revenue structure. Second was the judiciary provision whereby the geographic distribution, the method of selection and the definition of duties of judges were woefully behind the times. Third was the provision whereby the legislature met only every other year. A biennial assembly was workable when Illinois was an underpopulated wilderness without a transportation system but scarcely adequate for the nation's fourth biggest state under conditions when inflation made two-year budgetting impractical.

All this would have been enough reason for revising the constitution but there was also another one which made revision at once more necessary and more difficult. This was the very procedure provided for revision or amendment. An amendment to the Illinois constitution required first a two-thirds majority in both houses before it could even be submitted to the voters. To become law, it then required a majority of all votes cast in the general election at which the item was submitted. Since an amendment was rarely brought forcibly to the voters' attention beforehand, it was usually ignored on the ballots, and hence doomed to certain defeat. In order to revise the constitution itself, an even more cumbersome procedure was required. First a two-thirds majority in both houses had to favor a referendum on the subject of holding a constitutional convention. Then voters in the statewide referendum had to vote to hold it.

Stevenson started off by trying to push through a bill calling for a constitutional convention. This promptly encountered substantial opposition. Part of it came from those who feared that the revised constitution might — although the Governor offered assurances to the contrary — result in a state income tax. Part of it was apparently mere political contrariness, since several Republicans who had voted for the constitutional convention referendum during the Green regime, voted against it during Stevenson's. The bill passed the House but appeared likely to fail by a few votes in the Senate. There now arose a political dilemma.

One of the more colorful minor subdivisions in the Illinois State Legislature is a group of five legislators from Chicago's river wards, known collectively as "the West Side Bloc." The Pericles of the West Side Bloc is James J. Adduci whose qualifications for law-making include having been arrested eighteen times between 1920 and 1933 without ever having been convicted of anything.

For perhaps understandable reasons, the members of this colorful group, who emphasized their unanimity of purpose by attending sessions of the legislature in similar brightly patterned Hawaiian sports shirts, were adversely disposed toward a bill then pending, of which the purpose was to strengthen Chicago's Grand Jury procedure. Grapevine information revealed to Stevenson that, by promising to veto the crime commission bill, he could secure the West Side Bloc's support for the constitutional convention referendum. Later on, another even easier way to pass the constitutional conventional resolution was suggested to him. This was merely to agree not to veto a bill to permit dog racing in Illinois, in case the bill passed both houses, which was by no means likely. Stevenson rejected both propositions and the constitutional convention, with the West Side Bloc solidly against it, lost by five votes in the House.

With the constitutional convention defeated, Stevenson next announced his support of an amendment which might, to some degree, serve the same purpose. This was the "Gateway Amendment," so called because it provided a gateway to constitutional changes by permitting three amendments to be presented to the voters at once, instead of only one every two years, and by requiring a two-thirds majority of all those voting on each amendment instead of a majority of all votes cast. By calling a meeting of top leaders of both houses, the Governor got a bipartisan committee to back the gateway bill and eventually pushed it through both houses with Republican help. The gateway amendment, which provides the basis for further constitutional revisions, was itself the first amendment to the constitution passed in Illinois since 1908.

In attempting to withdraw from the presidential race last spring, Stevenson spoke of "my desire and the desire of many who have given me their help and confidence in our unfinished work in Illinois." A good many politicians on the national scene are just as puzzled by such utterances as the state politicians were by Stevenson when he took office in 1948. Stevenson, however, regards the gateway amendment as well as some of his other reforms, as chiefly significant in providing a chance to effect much bigger improvements in state government during the next four years. He is aware that a hurriedly picked successor, to get elected at all, might have to make commitments that he himself can presumably get elected without making. Conversely, he fears that without his presence in Springfield, even such a rudimentary reform as the merit system for the state police might easily be subject to immediate repeal and the rest of his hard-won program speedily ruined.

Another four-year term at the Executive Mansion seems to Stevenson not merely insurance against ruin of the work already accomplished. It also offers a chance to make the Illinois government into an approximation of what he thinks state government ought to be. As a devotee of decentralization of authority. Stevenson sees a deep national significance in such an achievement. If he could make it, his conscience might well permit him to consider his present job finished, and to start in on a bigger one, if the occasion arose.

9

During the period of the Stevenson presidential boom, one of the out-of-town political observers who dropped in to survey the Springfield scene was a pundit from Montana. After a week of talking to Stevenson and his administrative assistants, the visitor sought out one of the Chicago reporters assigned to the capital.

"This Stevenson," said the visitor, "he seems to be surrounded by a lot of well-scrubbed college boys and I've seen all of them. Now, who the hell do you go to around here when you want to talk politics?"

The effect made by Stevenson's entourage upon a pundit judging it by Helena standards was perhaps understandable. Notably absent from the Governor's staff is anything remotely like a Jim Farley, a Louis Howe or even a Harry Hopkins. Outside of Colonel Arvey, who, when not in Chicago, now spends most of his time in Florida, the only member of the Governor's staff with extra-parochial political connections is a young man named Richard Nelson, whose gray hair belies both his age, which is thirty five, and his role on the national scene, which is that of President of the Young Democrats of America. Partly in an effort to keep up his out-of-state contacts, Nelson quite often accompanies the Governor to his more distant speaking engagements. "The truth is," says Nelson, who nurses no illusions about his role on such excursions, "that I have probably sat at the extreme left-end of more daises than anyone else of my age in America. I always expect to get pushed off at any moment, and I wouldn't be surprised to find that one of my legs had grown longer than the other."

Along with McGowan, Blair and Nelson, the Governor's circle of administrative aides, includes Don Hyndman, a forty-two-year old alumnus of the Associated Press, who handles much of the Governor's official correspondence and does most of the research for his speeches; William Flanagan, another ex-newspaperman and public relations expert, who acts as press-secretary; Lawrence E. Irvin, a native of Bloomington and an ex-Red Cross Field director who handles personnel and runs the administrative offices; and Ross Randolph, the latest recruit to the staff, an ex-FBI man who specializes in investigating the investigating staffs — whose lapses, in the matter of cigarette taxes and horse-meat hamburgers, have been the administration's most serious failures to date.

This staff, which meets with the Governor for a three-hour conference every Thursday morning, has a by no means accidental resemblance to the group of political disciples which has surrounded Tom Dewey, as district attorney and later as governor of New York. Stevenson is an admirer of Dewey methods in state government and has carefully studied his handling of state hospitals, prisons, roads and insurance supervision. Early last winter Robert E. Dineen, Dewey's former insurance superintendent, who resigned to become vice-president of Northwestern Mutual Life, paid a visit to Springfield where he and Edward Day, who heads the Illinois Department of Insurance, addressed a convention of insurance agents. Before the meeting, Day took Dineen to the Governor's office where the Governor quizzed him for an hour asking him how Dewey's personal staff was organized, how many aides there were, how their work was divided, what salaries they got and how many secretaries were assigned to each.

Day himself is an alumnus of Stevenson's corps of administrative assistants, as is Judge Walter Schaefer, a one-time Northwestern University law professor who was subsequently elevated to justice of the state supreme court and has been widely mentioned as a possible successor to Stevenson in the event of his own graduation to larger endeavors. Other star members on the roster of department heads are Joseph Pois of Finance, a Chicago Ph.D. who had held wide and highly remunerative posts in private industry before coming to Springfield; and Fred K. Hoehler of Public Welfare, who headed UNRA's displaced persons division in Europe and renewed a previous acquaintance with Stevenson in London.

One of the well-known difficulties of national, let alone state, administration, is getting top-notch people for jobs which offer little financial incentive and at best a brief premium in prestige. In bringing to Springfield executives of a standard well above that of the Washington average, Stevenson's own wide acquaintance in high level business and bureaucratic circles has been advantageous, as has been the consequent, reciprocal confidence of appointees in his administration. Hoehler, for example, agreed to join the welfare department on a three-month basis, to devise an over-all plan for cleaning up the mental hospitals. Once started, he stayed on because he found the job was free from the pressures of politics and patronage. "I've been in this sort of thing all my life," Hoehler said recently, "but I could see that this set-up was something entirely new. It's hard to explain to an outsider who doesn't know state politics. I do know them and I had never seen anything at all like this before. There was a job that could really be done here; that interested me, so I never got around to leaving."

So far as Stevenson's availability for the presidency is concerned, the availability to him as governor of such executives as Hoehler has, ironically, become a handicap. The Governor is well aware that, under the circumstances, political pressures to which he is immune would be applied to any one who succeeded him. His loyalty to the people for whose careers he feels responsible, as well as to his legislative program, have thus been among his major explicit motives for preferring Springfield to the White House. By the same token, of course, if Stevenson had gone to the Senate instead of the state capital in 1948, he would never have had the administrative experience that is now one of his chief qualifications for an even bigger executive job.

Among the many other reasons advanced by outsiders to explain the Governor's reluctance to leave Springfield, possibly the least convincing is the notion that, while the presidency is a stupendous job for anyone, it might be beyond the powers of a chief executive not equipped with a wife to relieve him of the social side of the burden. As a lifelong trouble-shooter by temperament as well as talent, and one whose skill in this specialty has now reached Herculean heights, the Governor tends to be delighted rather than dismayed by occupational difficulties. One of the things that enables him to enjoy his stern curriculum in the Springfield Executive Mansion is that it too offers just such a double burden, which he has learned not only to carry but to juggle.

Like most politicians, the Governor is intensely gregarious. The lively correspondence which he keeps up with his friends is full of threats to have this or that one of them pulled into the Mansion by the state police unless they offer to come of their own accord. Partly on this account, and partly because of the traditional exigencies of political entertaining, the Mansion is run less like an ordinary private house than a sort of cross between a convention hotel and a tourist museum. During the regime of Henry Horner, also a bachelor, a tradition grew up whereby various ladies' organizations in and around Springfield were encouraged to use the first-floor rooms of the Mansion for teas, musicales and occasional soireés. This practice continued under Governor and Mrs. Green with the result that it is now a rare week when one or more such group fails to swarm up the drive and into the Mansion's receiving rooms. As a rule, the Governor drops in on these gatherings for a few minutes but if he wants to reach the third flood without getting involved, he can do so surreptitiously by means of an elevator that runs direct from the office to his bedroom. Like the parties it enables him to duck, the elevator is a bequest from Horner, who had it installed during his long illness.

While usually a convenience, the elevator has sometimes proved to be the opposite as on one occasion during Stevenson's first year in office when his guest of honor at the Mansion was Carl Sandburg. Aware that Sandburg wanted to sleep late, the Governor moved out of his own room so that the great poet could have the most comfortable quarters in the house in which to do so. Also present at the time were Stevenson's youngest son, John Fell, then eleven, and a small contemporary, who decided it would be fun to inspect the celebrity in his slumbers and figured that they could easily manage it by riding up in the elevator and peaking through the window. Unfortunately, the window was higher than they were, which led to some scrambling around in the car and a breakdown of its mechanism. Sandburg was awakened betimes by repairmen who were obliged to traverse his room in order to extract the occupants.

When Stevenson was working on Navy labor relations during the war, one of his associates was the Chicago *Daily New's* top labor reporter, Edwin Lahey. Lahey, who rejoined the *News* after the war, last spring wrote a biographical series about the Governor in which he said: "He knows his sprawling two-billion-dollar organization the way a country storekeeper knows where the last stray card of safety pins is stored." This may be something of an overstatement but Stevenson does show a kind of affectionate zeal toward the minutiae of his job that sometimes bewilders visitors who, after they have been inveigled into paying a visit at the Mansion, find themselves left to their own devices while the Governor toils away in his cellar.

Some months ago, an old friend of Stevenson's, visiting him for a few days, became seriously concerned over the Governor's habit of returning to work after dinner, and interrupted him at about eleven o'clock, to tell him so.

"Now just an example," said the friend, "what is that paper you have in your hand right now? I'll bet even money it's something someone else could just as well be doing for you."

"Well, to tell you the truth," said Stevenson, "it's about the contract specifications for some insulation to go around pipes in the basement of one of the buildings at the Manteno State Hospital."

"Exactly," said the friend, "that's what I mean. You ought to delegate a job like that. You're no expert on pipe insulation."

"Of course not," said Stevenson, "but that's just why I'm looking this thing over. I wanted to find out about it."

During the height of the excitement last April, when Stevenson had been answering two or three calls a minute on the subject of his presidential plans, he received one from Joseph Gill, who replaced Colonel Arvey as Chairman of the Cook County Democratic Committee when the latter became a national committeeman. Stevenson and Gill conversed for upward of half an hour. The principal subject of their talk was a $6,500 a year employee in a state bureau who, the Governor thought, might be more advantageously situated elsewhere in a different post, at that time occupied by a man who was having a fight with his superior. The new job was in many ways better than the old one, but it only paid $6,000 a year. What did Gill think about this? Would the pay cut create a hardship? Did he agree with the Governor's conclusions about the proficiencies of the two men involved? Gill proposed a new solution, involving a third state employee. The Governor knew all about him also and countered with some reservations. The talk went on for half an hour on this, and related topics. When it ended, in a mutually acceptable decision, Stevenson hung up the receiver reluctantly.

"Well thank you for calling, Joe," he said. "I certainly enjoy talking to you. I'd rather talk to you than almost anyone. You don't know how much good it does me."

Only more astonishing than the rapidity with which the Stevenson-for-President boom had burgeoned in January was the rapidity with which it withered in April, after Stevenson's statement of the reasons why he "could not accept a nomination." What made the latter phenomenon so surprising was that, granting that there was at least some reason for the boom, there seemed to be very little for its termination — save the customary reluctance of professional politicians to acquaint themselves with the real facts of the matter.

The facts were simple enough.

If Stevenson had announced, shortly after the famous Blair House meeting with Truman, that he wanted a presidential nomination, it would have contradicted his previous announcement that he was seeking a second term as governor. In addition to being out of character, such a contradiction would have been so frivolous as, incidentally, to have endangered Stevenson's chances of getting a nomination — since there were no concrete developments to which he could have attributed his sudden change of mind.

The passage of time not only failed to provide any such developments but also in itself strengthened rather than weakened Stevenson's prior commitments to the state of Illinois. For him to have repudiated these commitments in response to a mere hue and cry about the possibility of a presidential nomination would have been frivolous at the outset. It would have been unpardonable after the commitments had acquired added force from usage.

If it became increasingly hard for Stevenson to release himself from his commitments completely at any given point in time, it was always wholly impossible for him to release himself from them to a limited degree.

As he himself has pointed out, a statement to the effect that he would accept a nomination but not campaign for it would have been tantamount to starting a campaign.

Likewise, any indication, however indirect, that he could "accept a draft," would under the circumstances have meant that the draft was actually nothing of the sort.

In addition to belying his commitments fully as much as an openly avowed candidacy, either of these two methods would have been additionally distasteful to Stevenson and disadvantageous to his candidacy, in being markedly devious.

There was in fact only one time when Stevenson could, with any propriety whatever, have declared himself for the presidency. That was before he had declared himself for governor. Even then the propriety would have been questionable on other grounds, since no one had suggested that he do such a thing.

Stevenson's April 16th statement, in short, was dictated by circumstances. But even assuming that he not only had to make it but that he also wanted to make it, the statement, in the nature of things, was not binding upon anyone.

In saying that he "could not" accept a presidential nomination, Stevenson was merely acknowledging an obligation from which he was powerless to release himself. He *could* however be released from the obligation by others than himself—specifically by the members of the Democratic National Convention.

When an officer is promoted, his new responsibilities preclude his former ones. Likewise, a politician's loyalty to the whole country must exceed his duty to any part of it. To be sure, there was only one way to find out whether Stevenson would accept a draft. That was to draft him. But the real uncertainty was less whether it was his duty to accept a draft than whether it was the convention's duty to find out.

As to this, opinions naturally varied, but certain facts at least were plain. The American two-party system operates on a simple principle. Each party puts up its best candidate and the country chooses between them.

There seemed little question that Stevenson — judged by any criterion applicable to presidential possibilities — was the best candidate available in the Democratic Party.

The questions that confronted the Democratic National Convention were, therefore, only two. One was whether it really wanted the best; and the other was whether, if it did want the best, it had the courage and the common sense to get it.

Part Two

1

IN THE FOREGOING chapters, an effort has been made to tell something of Adlai Ewing Stevenson's origins, environment and experience. No effort has been made to express, interpret or appraise his opinions upon controversial issues. Such expression would have seemed gratuitous because the Governor has already spoken for himself. Interpretation seemed unnecessary because Stevenson speaks explicitly. As for appraisal, that may more justly be left to the reader.

Many of Stevenson's opinions were expressed before they became a matter of national concern. Many of them by corollary were made to relatively small gatherings and received relatively scant attention. What follows, therefore, is a collection of Stevenson's utterances — speeches, excerpts from speeches, writings and informal conversations—intended to provide a cross section of his thinking. The first item is a speech delivered by the Governor at Northwestern University's Founders' Day — January 21st, 1951.

In reading a speech, or for that matter anything else, the occasion of its composition must be taken into account; not to do this is at best to miss its full value and at worst to misunderstand it entirely. Everyone understands the danger of quoting bits of an argument out of context; but to consider a speech in full without considering the circumstances that prompted it is to take the whole speech, as it were, out of context.

Northwestern is one of eight institutions (the others are Illinois Wesleyan, Illinois College, Bradley University, Centre College, Lake Forest College, Hampden-Sidney College and McKendree College) from which Stevenson holds honorary degrees. To mark the occasion of Founders' Day, the university had invited George F. Kennan and Reinhold Niebuhr to speak on specific subjects relating to the state of the world at that point in its history. Stevenson had been asked to deal with world affairs in a general way, so as to set the tone and establish a framework for the remarks of Kennan and Niebuhr.

January 21st, 1951, was not only the 100th anniversary of Northwestern; it was also a year to the day before Stevenson's somewhat more topical address to the Urban League, which, indirectly, made him a national figure. In 1951, Stevenson was still just a state governor and only beginning to be marked as an exceptionally effective one. Disturbing events were at the foreground of national attention. The Chinese had launched their attack across the Yalu River a few weeks before; MacArthur was being criticized for failing to stop them. On the home front, the Kefauver investigation had started to make headlines; juke boxes were playing the Ten-

nessee Waltz. The nation was in the midst of the so-called
Great Debate on foreign policy, to which the Governor's
speech was—in the context of the immediate news—a rather
minor footnote. Stevenson said:

Some five years ago this university, for reasons best known
to its trustees, conferred an honorary degree on me. Having
thus honored me I suppose the least the Governor of Illinois
could do in appreciation was to decline President Miller's and
Mr. Burgess' invitation to speak at this 100th anniversary
convocation. Instead I accepted, after the manner of insensi-
tive and egotistical politicians. I apologize.

Because there are others who can speak with authority
about the founding of Northwestern University, I am, with,
I am sure, your enthusiastic approval, going to resist the
temptation to tell you of the faith and convictions of the
founders who stood here 100 years ago and dreamed of "a
university of the highest order of excellence." All that we
see about us testifies that they founded well and that their
successors have wrought well upon those foundations. In the
100 years the dream by the lake here in Dr. Evans' town
has become one of the world's large and honored communities of scholars.

Early Illinois was notoriously inhospitable to higher education and I recall the remark of a lusty legislator who said in
opposition to a bill to charter the first three Illinois schools
that he was "born in a briar thicket, rocked in a hog trough
and never had his genius cramped by the pestilential air of
a college."

Northwestern, too, was born upon a scene on which the

light of higher education shone but fitfully. But in our time one never sees a considered catalogue of the assets of Illinois that does not always proudly list its universities at the top.

I once heard it said that Massachusetts Institute of Technology "humanized the scientist" while Harvard "simonized the humanist." Just what Northwestern does I don't know; perhaps both. But at all events its contributions to the sciences and the humanities and also to the wholesome goodness and gaiety we associate with American student life have brought to this campus imperishable distinction and affection.

Thanks to Northwestern, its neighbor, the University of Chicago, the great State University, and many distinguished lesser institutions, Illinois, and particularly this section of the state, is now one of the treasure houses, one of the major repositories, of the Western world's culture.

It is proper, therefore, that we pause to note the 100th birthday of this proud university; that we pause a moment in our feverish defense preparations to recall what we are defending. Certainly one of the things we are defending is the future security and health of privately supported universities such as Northwestern. In turn we confidently expect them to defend for generations to come the spirit of free inquiry and fearless scholarship which is a basic condition of free men. For that protection and for the contribution of the universities to "a large resolute breed of men" which Walt Whitman called the only bar against tyranny, we will have to trust to the future; we will have to trust that the guardians here and elsewhere of the riches of our learning will never forget what the treasure they guard is, what it is composed of. We will have to trust that the guardians of Western thought will never permit its vitality and beauty to be smothered by strong, arrogant men who burn books and bend thought to their liking, nor obscured by timid men trembling in the darkness of anxiety.

The continuity of our heritage of scholarship, both bold and free, which is the peculiar and priceless possession of the university, must, then, be entrusted to the future. But what of the present which has such a bearing on the health and strength and continuity of the custodians of our culture?

Are the universities to be stripped of students in order to defend our cultural heritage? The young of college age are the seed corn of a society and a nation. To survive must we eat our seed corn? And if we do, can we survive? We must and we will, I think, find at least a partial answer to that disturbing question. And we will find it in calm deliberation, not in frantic fright.

Then, like you, after some experience, I have made the disturbing observation that absence of thought in war seems to be mandatory. And, of course, total abstinence from thought is very agreeable for most of us, and a uniformly popular condition among adolescents. But is it necessary in mobilization, in half war, if you please? Perhaps we have something to think about here as we enter the new and unexplored era of the garrison state.

Again, I must ask with a shudder if it will be largely women who enjoy the benefits of more advanced education in the new era? Is the ancient tradition of masculine primacy in jeopardy? Heaven forbid! And I should think a little reflection on this appalling possibility by the male leaders in all countries could do more to insure peace than a balance of power in the world. It is high time, it seems to me, that we males begin to think of survival in terms of gender as well as nationality and ideology.

Northwestern was born here in a quiet village on Lake Michigan by a burgeoning city a hundred years ago. In 1851 Illinois was filling up with immigrants from the south and east. A steel plow to cut the tough prairie sod had been invented. The reaper had come to our prairies. On plank roads Illinois was rising out of the mud. A railroad was pushing westward. Europe was in political and economic ferment. The Irish and the Germans were coming in search of something better and more hopeful for the average man. With not 30,000 souls Chicago was struggling out of the swamps. Illinois was passing from the log cabin frontier era and shouldering its way into the new industrial day that was breaking upon the Union.

A hundred years have passed; a hundred years which have seen the culmination of a great historic expansive movement of peoples from Europe to the West, and the conquest, development and integration into the world community of the two great American continents, severed by revolutions but tied by cultural inheritance to their western European roots.

At the same time there came another great expansion — from West to East. The Slavic peoples and culture pushed through the Ural Mountains, across the vastness of Siberia to the Pacific and on across the Bering Sea to Alaska and our own West coast. The Russian tide collided with the Japanese, just emerging from the hermit's hut with vaulting ambitions too. There it stopped — for a time — but the land mass over which the Russian expansion surged has for the most part remained firmly in Russian hands, while the European overseas expansion created a new and independent center of power here on our continent.

Twice in 25 years our new center of power, stretching from the tropics to the Arctic and facing both the Pacific and the Atlantic, has been compelled to intervene to redress the balance of power in the world. And now with Britain and France enfeebled by these wars, with the German and Japanese power crushed, the United States and Russia, which have risen from the mists of these short hundred years, even as this university, stand face to face, with the other nations polarized around them, drawn by the gravitational pulls of proximity, coercion, self-interest and kinship.

Believing as we do in a community of free nations and free peoples acting peacefully and responsibly through governments freely chosen, we conclude at last that we cannot live in comfortable security with a great imperial power which has seen the barriers to its expansion collapse and is on the move again, taking here, probing there, and pressing relentlessly against the uncommitted, discontented millions. Capitalizing the ancient racial zenophobia and the messianic zeal to missionize the world of the Russian people, the leaders of the new Russia, armed with force and the old weapon of fomented revolution, use the seductive new weapon of communism to soften their victims. But whatever the trappings, the methods, the weapons, the objective is domination — imperialism. I often think it would be both more accurate and more effective if we talked less of communism with all its appeal for ignorant, miserable peoples and more of imperialism which threatens the freedom and independence of everyone and has no appeal. Communism can be a fighting faith, but imperialism is subtle slavery.

So, as Northwestern University enters its second century, America, rich, peaceful and undisciplined, finds itself face to face across both the seas with an inscrutable, ruthless conqueror, strong, cunning and armed with an egalitarian idea that has great appeal for the miserable masses of humanity. No longer is there anyone to protect us. No longer can we sow when and where we are certain to reap. There is no safe investment, no certain harvest any longer. We cannot even measure the price of saving ourselves. Indeed, we seem to be in some doubt as to whether we should save ourselves at all; whether we are worth the cost!

The quiet past in which this great university grew to manhood is no more. Our bright land is troubled and sorely tried. Things are badly out of balance when we spend $230 million for one aircraft carrier, four times the endowment of this university. Its future is in doubt. Our future is in doubt. Some say fight now. Some say despotism is the wave of the future. Some say abandon Asia. Some say abandon Europe. And worst of all, everybody says something — including me!

In our time peace has become as abnormal as war used to be because this is the revolution. And revolution is extremely irritating, vexatious and bewildering to a prosperous, peaceful, contented people that want nothing except to be left alone.

How have we reacted to this condition of perpetual danger? It seems to me that for five years we have suffered from the confusion and distraction of alternate moments of illusion and despair. Hoping always for a cheap and painless escape from the realities of a distasteful destiny, aided and abetted by politicians who will say anything to be popular and by editors either myopic or worse, public opinion has moved in violent pendular swings between optimism and pessimism, between the mountains of complacency and the marshes of despair.

In fatuous haste to be shut of war, worry and expense, we obliterate our power and leave it to the United Nations to keep a peace that never existed. When things go right we we gush paeans of praise for the United Nations; when they go wrong we damn it and even propose to forsake the good because it is not the perfect. In fear we overestimate the danger; imperil our liberties, exaggerate the foe's cunning and strength; even demand a showdown as though the certainty of doom were preferable to the uncertainty. Again, perpetual danger invites the complacency of status and we underestimate the peril by overconfidence in our virtue and power, as though that were enough in a moral contest. But the self hypnosis of loud and repeated talk about our right-eousness and freedom will rally no allies nor blow the Kremlin walls down.

And now as things get tough and we find we can't buy, threaten or preach our way to peace, we are menaced by amateur strategists. Even the isolationists have reappeared, flexing their muscles, or rather their tongues, and proclaiming "Let the whole world go. We should worry. We can defend ourselves with a strong navy and air force." Haven't they heard about Pearl Harbor or the atom bomb? Was the last war all in vain? Haven't they heard that we are not self-sufficient? Won't a garrison state become a police state? And do they forget that nothing succeeds like success? If they do, conquerors don't. I suppose any moment even America First may emerge full blown again, except that I hope this time it is more properly entitled American Last — last on the Kremlin's list.

The re-emergence of the straight isolationist doctrine —the same people saying the same things we heard before the whirlwind a decade ago — is to me the great regurgitation. They remind me of Charles Lamb's remark: "I cannot make present things present to me."

But fortunately the great debate about foreign policy, which was mostly a debate about military strategy and not foreign policy, appears to be about over. And, none too soon, it appears that we have about made up our mind to stop fighting each other, gather all the like-minded allies we can find and settle down seriously to the very serious business of getting stronger than the brigands that are preying on the world.

Perhaps an occasional national debate like this one is a healthy thing. It clears the air, releases tensions, focuses torpid attention on great issues, and melts divisionist controversy into a mould of common conviction.

Maybe we have about reached a common conviction that peace through power is our salvation. Maybe we have decided that only by once again redressing the balance of power in the world and confronting Russia with a preponderance of force can we thwart an imperialism more sinister than the world has ever seen.

But we should profit from an experience like this, because it won't be the last time we get rattled; it won't be the last time we doubt our beliefs and believe our doubts.

I suppose, for example, we will have to assume that the isolationist argument will have at least nine lives, for the very human reason that it pleases the average man because it spares him any immediate inconvenience or sacrifice, and it flatters his sense of power to feel that America can live alone and like it.

And have we learned that while the whole nation may debate the broad policy of whether to defend or not to defend, whether to defend alone or with allies, the details of the where, when and how we will defend are sometimes questions of military, political and diplomatic strategy which cannot be settled safely or wisely by public debate? Nor can they be wisely settled by men who behave, to borrow a line from King Lear, "as if they were God's spies," but who are neither military strategists nor geopoliticians.

Have we learned that what 160 million Americans know about our plans the enemy knows too? Have we learned that hunting scapegoats is not a foreign policy?

Have we learned that our mission is the prevention, not just the survival of a major war? Have we discovered that there are no Gibraltars, no fortresses impregnable to death or ideas, any more?

While the debate talks incessantly in terms of our national crisis and our national survival, it is not just our crisis, it is the crisis of the whole free world. Have we learned that making domestic political capital out of world crisis is not the way to win friends and influence people? Do we realize that the Russians have already gained a portion of their objective by using our indecision and moral confusion to weaken our leadership in the free world? The Russians know the value of even reluctant allies in this final struggle for power. Do we? Or are we going to risk the slow strangulation that comes from whittling away the friendly world?

If we have not learned that having the most to lose we have the most to save, then, I say, let us pray.

But if we have, if the immensity of the responsibility and the stakes has dawned upon us, then the great debate has been a great blessing and we are on the way to thwart this latest greatest threat to all this university symbolizes.

Why should we be poor in spirit? The task is great, the price is high, but the prize is better than life. With Europe and its great industrial concentration and forward bases shored up and steadfast, with access to the tin and rubber of south Asia, middle eastern oil, African manganese and uranium, the scales are still weighted to the West, and the waves of the future are still free. Aggression must be called aggression in the United Nations. But in insisting on no equivocation about the legal and moral position, we dare not forget that the allegiance of India, uncommitted to East or West, is the ultimate objective of both East and West in the Orient. And we dare not fall into the trap, the *oubliette*, Russia has prepared for us in China. War there will drain our resources and at the same time make China completely dependent militarily on Russia. With every Russian jet at least six Russians go along. A weakened China means a stronger Russia pressing from behind against Hong Kong, Indo China, South Asia, and finally India. Hounded by people of small vision and great emotion it will not be easy to withstand the pressure to help solve Russia's problems with China. And with us mired in the morass of the China mainland the Soviet could turn next summer to some unfinished business with Tito in Yugoslavia.

Pray heaven we can remember amid the discord and chagrin of defeat that military force alone cannot win the day for us in Asia. Our moral authority there is low because we are white and Asia is colored. Desperately poor, struggling to shake off the shackles of white colonialism, Asia is just now passing thru the era of revolution, independence and self-determination that swept the Western world long ago. It will take preat patience, great insight, great restraint for us who see the whole world in our own image and likeness to win confidence and faith in the great uncommitted areas of Asia. It can't be done with the white man's sword. But it can be done; they can be convinced that communist imperialism is not liberation but a more deadly enemy of normal aspirations for freedom and social justice than colonialism.

Are we, I wonder, moving as a nation from our Greek period to our Roman period; from a period in which the validity of our ideas was the important consideration to one in which their effectiveness is crucial? Good intentions and reliance on the rightness of our cause will avail us little against an enemy that cares nothing about validity and is concerned only with effectiveness. The Greeks were right, but they died.

A danger greater, it seems to me, than Germany or Japan in the last war, or Communist imperialism now is moral fatigue, disintegration, half loyalty, timid faith — the "weakening of the central convictions to which Western man hitherto has pledged allegiance."

When freedom didn't exist it too was a fighting faith that

men would die for. But now that it is old, it looks a little pale and gentle and lacks the appeal to the militant, irrational sentiments once mobilized by conquering religions and now by imperial communism.

But communism resolves no anxieties. It multiplies them. It organizes terror. It is without spiritual content or comfort. It provides no basic security. In the long run it cannot cure the disease of this anxious age. But its short term methods are grimly effective. We can't sit still and wait for the fever to run its course. Without combative faith in our spiritual heritage, we won't long hold out against the subtleties of selfishness and fear. If Western civilization is to save its body, it must save its soul too. It must awake again the emotionalism, the confidence, the defiant faith of a resolute breed of men to whom liberty and justice mean something positive every day — not just when war has reduced us to the stark issue of self-preservation.

It's easy to care mightily then; it's hard now. It's easier to fight for principles than to live up to them. But now is the time that a passionate belief counts if we are to avoid another war, and if we are to avoid the greater menace of cowardly surrender to our own doubts and fears.

Don't the universities have a large, indeed the leading, role to play in articulating the purpose and the combative faith of a great people in this era of convulsive transition and this hour of discord and doubt? Don't they know best what we stand to lose?

We have proclaimed our military weakness, our vacillation, our hesitation, our fear. Enough of that! The test of a nation is defeat. The time has come to proclaim our faith in all its might and majesty. History will go on and "The Forfeiture of Freedom" would be a sorry title to this chapter; rather the historian must write that in arousing America to re-define and defend its ideals the ugliest despotism dug its grave in the twentieth century.

It was in 1776 that Tom Paine wrote: "The heart that feels not now is dead; the blood of his children will curse his cowardice, who shrinks back at a time when little might have saved the whole."

Stevenson's speech at Northwestern, like all the Governor's full-dress efforts in this line, was written by himself and delivered from a carefully revised text. A speech of a very different type was delivered by the Governor in May of 1950, when President Truman stopped off in Chicago to attend the Jefferson Jubilee in the Chicago Stadium. Where the audience in the Northwestern Chapel had been nonpartisan, small and intellectually well-versed in the Governor's subject matter, the stadium audience was huge (20,000), partisan and excited about hearing the President. The occasion called for an apparently extemporaneous introduction along the lines of the ones that Stevenson had provided so frequently and expertly at the Council on Foreign Relations. Stevenson spoke, from a floodlighted box, as follows:

Mr. President, we welcome you to Illinois which gave Abraham Lincoln to the world — and many other men and women who have added luster to our nation's history — including the majority leader of the United States who is here tonight. But I dare not call him by name lest it be thought that there is something political about this celebration!

We are proud that Illinois and Chicago could be host to this celebration in honor of the immortal philosopher of democracy — Thomas Jefferson — for whom liberty meant not only freedom of the person, but freedom of the mind and spirit as well.

To do our reverent honor on the 150th anniversary of his election to the presidency, we meet in this hall which has witnessed in our own time so many fateful events in American history — including a hot night just six years ago when a senator from Missouri was nominated to be vice President of the United States. We are proud it happened here!

And, Mr. President, while we refresh our memory of Jefferson's firm faith in the people, in life, liberty and the pursuit of happiness for all alike, may I remind you that until two years ago only three men of the political faith of Jefferson had been elected Governor of Illinois since the Civil War. The first was John Peter Altgeld — the Eagle Forgotten — a German immigrant; the second was Edward F. Dunne, but one generation removed from the old sod of Ireland; the third was Henry Horner, son of an immigrant and beloved in the memory of all those here tonight. May I remind you, Mr. President, that John Peter Altgeld was a Protestant, that Edward F. Dunne was a Catholic, that Henry Horner was a Jew.

That is the American story; that was the dream of Thomas Jefferson. And here, Mr. President, in the City of Chicago, on the prairies of Illinois, his descendants believe in human freedom; we believe in equal opportunity for all; we believe in special privilege for none; we believe in the democratic institutions; we believe in our chief executive; we believe in you, Mr. President!

In the age old struggle against tyranny over the bodies and minds and the souls of men we know there can be no respite, no rest for you or for us.

For:

> "On the plains of hesitation
> Bleach the bones of countless thousands
> Who, on the eve of victory, rested —
> And resting, died."

As each day, in the tradition of Jefferson, you forge a broader shield for free men everywhere, we join our prayers to yours that out of the ugly clamor and conflict there will come your heart's desire and ours — peace on earth.

2

EFFECTIVENESS IN GOVERNMENT *entails self-expression in action as well as in words. In a gubernatorial position, such assertion and such action may be observed in two forms: legislation that originates in the administration, and the veto. Legislation, however, may be, and usually is, modified by the legislators and may also in any case, be best inspected in its own operative consequences. Stevenson's numerous veto messages, of which half a dozen follow, exhibit his prose style to excellent advantage. What is more to the point, they show his ideas not in the abstract but in action; for the difference between a veto and a speech is comparable to the difference between shadow boxing and having a fight.*

Each veto message is preceded by a brief summary of the background of the legislation involved and of the political significance of the veto itself.

The Broyles Bill

Most celebrated, quoted, and controversial of Stevenson's vetoes was that of the so-called Broyles Bill, introduced by Mr. Paul Broyles, an Illinois State Senator from the Southern town of Mount Vernon. Broyles had previously headed an Illinois equivalent of the House Un-American Activities Committee which inquired into subversive activities and in-

*fluences in Chicago generally, and the University of Chicago
in particular, in 1947. The bill was earnestly advocated by
Broyles not only on the assembly floor but in private consultation with the Governor. It was backed by the powerful
Illinois Department of the American Legion. It secured
further public endorsement when it was opposed, before the
senate sitting as a committee of the whole, by the state's top
Communist, a Negro named Claude Lightfoot, whose behavior became so objectionable that he had to be removed
by the sergeant-at-arms. The bill was passed 35 to 15 in the
senate and 87 to 15 in the house. The Governor's veto
message read as follows:*

I herewith return, without my approval, Senate Bill No.
102, entitled "An Act to protect against subversive activities
by making it a crime to commit or advocate acts intended to
effect the overthrow of the Government of the United States
or the State of Illinois or of any political subdivision thereof
by violence or other unlawful means, or to attempt or con-
spire so to do, by definint subversive organizations and making them illegal, by establishing procedures to insure the
loyalty of candidates for public office and of public officers
and employees, and providing for the enforcement of the
provisions of said Act, and providing penalties for the vio-
lation thereof."

I veto and withhold my approval from this bill for the
following reasons:

"The stated purpose of this bill is to combat the menace of
world communism. That the Communist party — and all it
stands for — is a danger to our Republic, as real as it is
sinister, is clear to all who have the slightest understanding

of our democracy. No one attached to the principles of our society will debate this premise or quarrel with the objectives of this bill.

Agreed upon ends, our concern is with means. It is in the choice of methods to deal with recognized problems that we Americans, in and out of public life, so often develop differences of opinion. Our freedom to do so is a great source of strength and, if not impaired by mistakes of our own, will contribute greatly to the ultimate confusion of the enemies of freedom.

The issue with respect to means raised by this bill has two aspects. One is the question of the need for it in relation to existing weapons for the control of subversives. The other is whether this addition to our arsenal may not be a two-edged sword, more dangerous to ourselves than to our foes.

Were the latter alone involved, I should hesitate to impose my judgment upon that of the majority of the General Assembly. But it is precisely because the evil at hand has long since been identified and provided against that we here in Illinois need not now do something bad just for the sake of doing something.

What are the facts with respect to need? On June 4 last, the Supreme Court of the United States affirmed the conviction of the twelve top leaders of the Communist party in the United States. They were indicted under the provisions of an Act of Congress (the so-called "Smith Act") for conspiring (1) to organize as the Communist party a society for the teaching and advocacy of the overthrow and destruction of the government of the United States (which by definition in the Act includes the governments of the states and their political subdivisions) by force and violence, and (2) to advocate and teach the overthrow of the government of the United States, as so defined, by force and violence.

Close upon the heels of this opinion, the federal government has moved to indict twenty-one more known Communist leaders. It is, of course, no secret that the Federal Bureau of Investigation has identified and has under observation virtually every member of the Communist party and every serious sympathizer, and is prepared to take such persons into custody on short notice.

But Senate Bill 102 is unnecessary not alone because of the federal anti-subversive law and activity, but because under the existing laws of Illinois it is now, and has been since 1919, a felony for any person to advocate the reformation or overthrow, by violence or other unlawful means, of the state or federal government, or to assist in the organization, or to become a member of, any organization dedicated to that objective. Our laws also prohibit the compensation from state funds of subversive employees or members of subversive organizations.

Indeed, it is ironic that the Ober law of Maryland, on which Senate Bill 102 is patterned, was itself an effort to make Maryland's sedition laws as comprehensive as Illinois'!

Senate Bill No. 102 makes it a felony to commit or attempt any act intended to overthrow by force the federal or state governments, or any of their political subdivisions; to advocate or teach the commission of such acts; or to have any connection with an organization devoted to such an objective. This approach parallels and duplicates criminal statutes of both the federal and state governments already in effect. Nor am I aware of complaints by any State's Attorneys throughout Illinois that our present sedition laws are insufficient.

Not only does Senate Bill No. 102 appear wholly unnecessary, but I agree with the Bar Associations that if the present sedition laws could be strengthened by expressly prohibiting the commission of acts as well as the advocacy thereof, this could best be accomplished by amending the existing laws rather than enacting new and more laws. Criminal laws, especially on subjects of vital importance, should not be confused by patchwork and duplication.

But it is in the enforcement provisions that I find this bill most objectionable. The Attorney General of Illinois is directed to appoint a Special Assistant Attorney General who must assemble and deliver to the State's Attorney of each county all information relating to subversive acts or activities within such county. The local State's Attorney then must present this matter to the Grand Jury. The Assistant Attorney General in Springfield must maintain complete records of all such information which may, with the permission of the Attorney General, be made public.

This transmission of such information and the subsequent presentation of it to the Grand Jury is mandatory under the Act — and covers in terms all information, however inconclusive or insignificant I know of no precedent of any such interference with the normal discretion accorded to a public prosecutor. One of the important responsibilities of State's Attorneys and one of the greatest protections of the citizen is the exercise of sound judgment in sifting the many rumors, charges and counter-charges which come to State's Attorneys' attention. This is true in the operation of the criminal laws generally, and it must, of necessity, be even more true when we are dealing with criminal laws relating in large degree to the state of men's minds.

I can see nothing but grave peril to the reputations of innocent people in this perpetuation of rumors and hearsay. When we already have sedition laws prohibiting the offenses to which these provisions relate, I see more danger than safety in such radical change in the administration of criminal justice.

Other substantive provisions in the bill are intended to assure the loyalty of the employees of the state government and its political subdivisions. All agencies of government must establish procedures to ascertain that there are no reasonable grounds to believe that any applicant for employment is committed, by act or teaching, to the overthrow of the government by force or is a member of an organization dedicated to that purpose. Thus, one who wishes to work for the state or to each in a school must himself carry the burden of proving the absence of any reasonable grounds for believe that he is subversive or even belongs to a subversive organization. The bill does not even require that the applicant for employment know the purpose of such an organization.

Provisions as to those already employed also shift the burden of proof to the employee. With all the mutitude of employing agencies throughout the State, each establishing its own rule and procedures for the enforcement of these provisions, it is easy to see what variations there might be and what possibilities for discrimination depending upon the wisdom and fairness of the particular employer.

By such provisions as these, irreparable injury to the reputation of innocent persons is more than a possibility, it is a likelihood. If this bill became law, it would be only human for employees to play safe and shirk duties which might bring upon them resentment or criticism. Public service requires independent and courageous action on matters which affect countless private interests. We cannot afford to make public employees vulnerable to malicious charges of disloyalty. So far as the employers are concerned— heads of departments and of schools and so on — the only safe policy would be timid employment practices which could only result in a lowering of the level of ability, independence and courage in our public agencies, schools and colleges.

Lastly, the bill provides that candidates for public office, other than offices for which an oath is prescribed by the Constitution, shall file an affidavit that he is not a subversive person. The Attorney General informs me that, despite the exception made, this requirement is of dubious constitutionality.

Does anyone seriously think that a real traitor will hesitate to sign a loyalty oath? Of course not. Really dangerous subversives and saboteurs will be caught by careful, constant, professional investigation, not by pieces of paper.

The whole notion of loyalty inquisitions is a natural characteristic of the police state, not of democracy. Knowing his rule rests upon compulsion rather than consent, the dictator must always assume the disloyalty, not for a few but of many,

ADLAI E. STEVENSON

and guard against it by continual inquisition and "liquidation" of the unreliable. The history of Soviet Russia is a modern example of this ancient practice. The democratic state, on the other hand, is based on the consent of its members. The vast majority of our people are intensely loyal, as they have amply demonstrated. To question, even by implication, the loyalty and devotion of a large group of citizens is to create an atmosphere of suspicion and distrust which is neither justified, healthy nor consistent with our traditions.

Legislation of this type, in Illinois and elsewhere, is the direct result of the menacing gains of communism in Europe and Asia. But it would be unrealistic, if not naive, to assume that such legislation would be effective in combatting Communist treachery in America. Such state laws have nowhere uncovered a single case of subversive disloyalty.

Basically, the effect of this legislation, then, will be less the detection of subversives and more the intimidation of honest citizens. But we cannot suppress thought and expression and preserve the freedoms guaranteed by the Bill of Rights. That is our dilemma. In time of danger we seek to protect ourselves from sedition, but in doing so we imperil the very freedoms we seek to protect, just as we did in the evil atmosphere of the alien and sedition laws of John Adams' administration and just as Britain did during the Napoleonic era. To resolve the dilemma we will all agree that in the last analysis the Republic must be protected at all costs, or there will be no freedoms to preserve or even regain. But if better means of protection already exist, then surely we should not further imperil the strength of freedom in search of illusory safety.

We must fight traitors with laws. We already have the laws. We must fight falsehood and evil ideas with truth and better ideas. We have them in plenty. But we must not confuse the two. Laws infringing our rights and intimidating unoffending persons without enlarging our security will neither catch subversives nor win converts to our better ideas. And in the long run evil ideas can be counteracted and conquered not by laws but only by better ideas.

Finally, the states are not, in my judgment, equipped to deal with the threat of the world Communist movement which inspired this bill. Communism threatens us because it threatens world peace. The great problems with which communism confronts us are problems of foreign relations and national defense. Our Constitution wisely leaves the solution of such matters to the national government.

In conclusion, while I respect the motives and patriotism of the proponents of this bill, I think there is in it more of danger to the liberties we seek to protect than of security for the Republic. It reverses our traditional concept of justice by placing upon the accused the burden of proving himself innocent. It makes felons of persons who may be guilty more of bad judgment than of anything else. It jeopardizes the freedom of sincere and honest citizens in an attempt to catch and punish subversives. It is unnecessary and redundant.

I know full well that this veto will be distorted and misunderstood, even as telling the truth of what I knew about the reputation of Alger Hiss was distorted and misunderstood. I know that to veto this bill in this period of grave anxiety will be unpopular with many. But I must, in good conscience, protest against any unnecessary suppression of our ancient rights as free men. Moreover, we will win the contest of ideas that afflicts the world not by suppressing these rights, but by their triumph. We must not burn down the house to kill the rats.

Public Housing Bill

In Illinois, as in many other states, public housing is a subject which creates acute tensions and sharp differences of opinion among many individuals who are affected for many different reasons. Real estate boards and associations are usually mobilized against public housing projects, as an invasion of private enterpirse. In individual neighborhoods, especially in urban ones, local economic units are affected favorably, or adversely by housing developments. They react accordingly. Finally, race hostilities are often aroused and may be then utilized by the other interested groups — especially when, for example, a low-cost development which may be largely tenanted by colored tenants, is adjacent to a locality already inhabited by some other closely-knit racial group. In Senate Bill 50, these motivations, especially the latter, were skillfully disguised under a façade purporting to make the issue one of "home-rule" and "local government." The bill provided, in effect, that housing site developments be approved by a referendum among the neighbors. The salient passages in the Stevenson veto read as follows:

This bill provides that no new Housing Authority may be created nor may a federally aided housing project be commenced or enlarged until approved by a majority of the voters residing within the area of operation, except that if the project is in Chicago the residents of a ward any part of which is within two miles of any part of such project can vote at the referendum.

It evidently is the legislative intent that, except in Chicago, all the voters resident in the city, village, etc. shall be eligible to vote upon the question.

However, in Chicago the vote on such questions is on the basis of all precincts in any ward, any part of which ward is within two miles of any part of such proposed project or proposed enlargement of an existing project.

Thus, an individual who lives in a ward, a part of which is within two miles of the project, is eligible to vote even though he may live five miles away from the project, if the ward is sufficiently elongated to give him this tenuous hold on suffrage. But another person living at the edge of a ward nearest to the project, yet just in excess of two miles from the project, is ineligible to vote.

This bill would negate the principle of representative government by requiring frequent referenda on detailed administrative matters, instead of on questions of broad public policy. Responsibility for providing low rent housing has been assigned to local housing authorities, subject to controls vested in the Public Housing Administration of the federal government, the State Housing Board, where state aid is involved, and the local municipal governing body. No program may go forward without the scrutiny and approval of the elected representatives of the people. The referendum method provided in this bill would substitute a town hall meeting for representative government and is neither wise nor practical on isolated issues, where the legislature has provided a system of checks and balances. It would enable an interested minority to organize the opposition of those who might be fearful of, or inconvenienced by a proposed housing project, thereby blocking an improvement which would be beneficial to the entire community.

This bill would retard the construction of urgently needed homes. Each new project, each new plan, each new site would require a separate interpretation to the voters. Experience has shown that every additional control affixed to the administration of the program has been at the expense of the results.

If the principle of this bill were sound, why should not we require a referendum within two miles of each proposed new school in the city of Chicago before it could be built? And should not the state then require a referendum within two miles of any airport? Should the residents immediately adjacent to Congress Street have to approve its construction? Should we require a referendum around each particular area where a park is to be located? Should the surrounding neighborhood vote on whether to have new police and fire stations, hospitals, streetcar barns, a library, a tuberculosis sanitarium, a post office? Would the sponsors of this principle want each neighborhood to vote on whether people from other neighborhoods could use its parks and libraries?

It would be a dangerous doctrine to say that a public improvement which by law and judicial interpretation is for a public purpose, is now of concern only to the people in the immediate surrounding neighborhood. Who is to determine where the limit of interest ends? If this theory were to prevail, why two miles? Why, one might ask, should it not be one house, or one block, or one hundred yards? To what extent would the sponsors of this Bill carry the notion that public improvements are only for the benefit, and therefore only the concern, of people in the immediate vicinity. Moreover, if this type of legislation were to become law in respect to low cost housing on what logical basis could the same right be withheld from the residents of areas to be redeveloped by private enterprise?

I think it unwise, indeed dangerous, to substitute government by referendum for government by representation even in this limited area. Nor can I approve such a transparent device to scuttle the low cost housing program and reverse the long-established public policy of the state.

Trailer Camp Bill

In Illinois, as elsewhere, trailer camps often constitute a nuisance, if not a health menace, to communities in which they are located. House bill 1104 provided a case where the real — not, as in the housing bill, the pretended — issue was local versus state government. Stevenson's views on this far-reaching subject are summarized in his veto.

I veto and withhold my approval from this bill for the following reasons:

This bill appropriates $86,000 to the Department of Public health to license and regulate trailer parks. I am vetoing this appropriation because I intend to veto House Bill No. 851 providing for such licensing and regulation.

ADLAI E. STEVENSON

I recognize that trailer camps have created a genuine public health problem which has become acute in several places in the state and requires regulation. At the same time I also find in these bills another example of the constant migration of local repsonsibility to higher levels of government. We will not arrest the concentration of governmental authority at points further and further removed from the people if we persist in passing legislation of this kind which is clearly usurpation by the state of what should be a function of local government.

If local government refuses to accept and discharge its responsibilities, the people will have only themselves to blame for the expansion of central, and the shrinkage and impotence of local, governments. While, as I say, I do not question the desirability, indeed the necessity, for the regulation here proposed, I emphatically disapprove the abdication of local responsibility for local problems. And I do not wish to be a party to what seems to me a wholly unnecessary extension of state services which can and should be performed locally by city or county governments.

Old Age Pensions

Illinois's 165,000 old age pensioners were greatly cheered in 1951 by the introduction of Senate Bill 556 which would have given them all a blanket 10 percent raise — and cost the state of Illinois $14,300,000. The bill was introduced by the late Wallace Thompson, the Senate's Republican leader — like Stevenson an example of "the better element" in politics and noted as a vigorus verbal proponent of economy in gov-

[148]

ernment. In fact, since the bill provided no means of revenue for the funds it proposed to disburse, it was less a contradiction of Thompson's stand on economy, than an effort to give the Governor a political black eye. Illinois old age pensioners — along with many of their relatives who naturally favor any economic benefits conferred on them — comprise a formidable political bloc. With not much to do except talk politics and preserve their rights, they have a Pensions' Union whose president, upon Stevenson's veto of this bill, announced that the first item on her subsequent order of business would be to defeat the Governor in his campaign for re-election. Stevenson could have ducked the punch and parried, by signing the bill and asking the Republicans who passed it to appropriate the necessary funds. Instead he wrote a veto message which included the following caustic paragraphs:

The effect of this item is to require the state to spend many millions of dollars in excess of estimated available funds. Its sponsors, who profess the virtues of fiscal responsibility, made no pretense of providing the necessary funds by increased taxes. Furthermore, the Public Aid Commission is already required by law and does adjust old age pensions and other public assistance grants periodically in accordance with fluctuations in the cost of living.

I can only assume, therefore, that the authors of this transparently political gesture were more concerned with raising the hopes of our aged dependents than their incomes. Perhaps such cynicism is good politics but it seems to me cruel as well as fiscally irresponsible — and, may I add, futile, to the extent that its objective was political intimidation of the Governor. Had the purpose been philanthropic rather than demagogic, the authors would also have at least covered the recipients of other forms of assistance. But the others, the dependent children and recipients of general relief, are not organized politically as some have pointed out.

Sunday Car Bill

In 1949, Stevenson vetoed a bill which would have fixed a minimum price for cigarettes, on the ground that the free enterprise system in general allows anyone to sell cigarettes, or any other legal commodity for a loss if he feels like it. In 1951, the Assembly passed Senate Bill 504, supported by the great majority of the state's second-hand car-dealers, which was aimed at those few among their competitors who, by their insistence on staying open on Sunday, forced all the rest to do likewise. The Governor's veto is noteworthy as a further definition and demonstration of his views on the meaty subject of economic restraints generally:

I veto and withhold my approval from this bill for the following reasons:

This bill makes it a criminal offense for any person to sell a motor vehicle on Sunday.

The Attorney General advises me that this bill is uncostitutional, and I append hereto a copy of his opinion to this effect.

I cannot forbear to add that this is one case in which the constitutional objection and sound policy clearly coincide.

Under this bill anyone who chooses to sell his automobile on Sunday could be imprisoned for as long as ninety days. Surely our public officials charged with law enforcement have more important tasks than to seek out and prosecute persons engaging in such transactions. If such a restriction on Sunday trade is sound for automobiles, why should it not be extended to newspapers, groceries, ice cream cones and other harmless commercial transactions? Carried to its logical extreme, any business group with sufficient influence in the legislature can dictate the hours of business of its competitors. And if hours, why not prices?

Under our free enterpices system government should not interfere by regulatory or prohibitory laws in the business field except (1) where the activity in question is directly related to the public health, safety, morals or welfare or (2) to *enforce* competition. Traffic in automobiles does not qualify under the one, and, so far as the latter is concerned, its only purpose and effect are to *restrain* competition.

Surely such restrictive legislation as this is not compatible with our earnest convictions and constant proclamations about the merits of free enterprise.

Log-rolling Bill

Legislative log-rolling — whereby one legislator gets others to vote for local improvements in his district on a reciprocal basis — is an ancient and transparent political device but one which enjoys a traditional acceptance in Congress as well as state legislatures. Stevenson vetoed all such bills (which would have involved total appropriations of some

ADLAI E. STEVENSON

$50,000,000) passed by the General Assembly and attached a succinct statement of his reasons for doing so in the case of Senate Bill 216:

I herewith return, without my approval, Senate Bill No. 210, entitled "An Act providing for the construction of a state highway bridge across the Illinois river at the city of Beardstown, and making an appropriation therefor."

I veto and withhold my approval from this bill for the following reasons:

The bill authorizes and *directs* the Department of Public Works and Buildings to construct a suitable highway bridge across the Illinois River at Beardstown, at such location as may be selected by the department; and appropriates $3,250,-000 from the Motor Fuel Tax Fund for this purpose.

The General Assembly long ago established the desirable policy of leaving the details of the expenditure of funds upon highway improvements to the Department of Public Works and Buildings. Under existing laws, the department has power and discretion to make expenditures from a general appropriation to it from the road fund, on the various classifications of highways specified in the statutes. If a particular improvement proposed is on one of such highways, the time, manner, and place of its construction are rightly left to the determination of the expert engineers of the Division of Highways.

This bill is a direct departure from this traditional — and wholly beneficial — practice. Its effect is to deny to the department the discretion it should exercise in formulating a program of highway improvements on the basis of scientific traffic counts and other professional methods of ascertaining priority in the spending of available funds.

Entirely apart from whether the department would be legally bound to carry out the direction contained in a bill of this nature, the approach is unsound. Illinois has suffered too much in the past from the construction of highway projects on a political, rather than on a traffic, basis.

People generally condemn the log-rolling, pork-barreling, and political back-scratching which have so long plagued the federal Congress in its appropriations for river and harbor and other internal improvements. We should avoid the same practices by a close and impartial scrutiny of the decisions of the department by the General Assembly and by all other citizens concerned with the efficient expenditure of public funds. But the evil so to be guarded against is only compounded by special bills of the kind under consideration.

It should be for the department to determine, without reference to any considerations other than the priority of relative need determined on a statewide basis, when a bridge should be built at Beardstown or any other place; and when that determination is made with respect to a location on a federal aid or state bond issue route, the department needs no special act like this one for authority to proceed. The program of construction for the next biennium published by the department already makes provision for a bridge at Beardstown on Federal Aid Route 4. If adequate highway funds are available — a matter to which the General Assembly is giving its attention currently — this Beardstown bridge will be built anyway. This fact only underscores my conclusion that, at best, legislation of this kind is superfluous. At the worst, as in the case of a bridge not having the priority of traffic need of the one at Beardstown, it is an unwarranted interference with any honest professional effort to spend highway funds for the benefit of *all* the citizens of Illinois.

There is also grave doubt as to the legality of this appropriation from the Motor Fuel Tax Fund. When considered in connection with the existing law with respect to the monthly allocations of the Motor Fuel Tax Fund, this appropriation creates difficulties that would probably require further legislative clarification.

There is another particular in which special bills of this character are undesirable. It is the custom of the General Assembly to appropriate for highway purposes for each biennium the amount of the anticipated revenues for highway construction and maintenance. If special project appropriations are passed, the funds appropriated are sterilized and cannot be used for other purposes even though the special project may not be constructed due to unforeseeable circumstances, such as a shortage of steel, for example.

Cat Bill

Next to Stevenson's veto of the Broyles Bill, his most quoted composition in this sympathetic literary form is probably that of a bill promulgated by Illinois bird-lovers, and passed by both houses in 1949:

I herewith return, without my approval, Senate Bill No. 93 entitled, "An Act to provide Protection to Insectivorous Birds by Restraining Cats." This is the so-called "Cat Bill."

I veto and withhold my approval from this bill for the following reasons:

It would impose fines on owners or keepers who permitted their cats to run at large off their premises. It would permit any person to capture, or call upon the police to pick up and imprison, cats at large. It would permit the use of traps. The bill would have statewide application — on farms, in villages, and in metropolitan centers.

This legislation has been introduced in the past several sessions of the legislature, and it has, over the years, been the source of much comment — not all of which has been in a serious vein. It may be that the General Assembly has now seen fit to refer it to one who can view it with a *fresh outlook*. Whatever the reasons for passage at this session, I cannot believe there is a widespread public demand for this law or that it could, as a practical matter, be enforced.

Furthermore, I cannot agree that it should be the declared public policy of Illinois that a cat visiting a neighbor's yard or crossing the highway is a public nuisance. It is in the nature of cats to do a certain amount of unescorted roaming. Many live with their owners in apartments or other restricted premises, and I doubt if we want to make their every brief foray an opportunity for a small game hunt by zealous citizens — with traps or otherwise. I am afraid this bill could only create discord, recrimination and enmity. Also consider the owners' dilemma: To escort a cat abroad on a leash is against the nature of the cat, and to permit it to venture forth for exercise unattended into a night of new dangers is against the nature of the owner. Moreover, cats perform useful service, particularly in rural areas, in combatting rodents — work they necessarily perform alone and without regard for property lines.

We are all interested in protecting certain varieties of birds. That cats destroy some birds, I well know, but I believe this legislation would further but little the worthy cause to which its proponents give such unselfish effort The problem of cat versus bird is as old as time. If we attempt to resolve it by legislation, who knows but what we may be called upon to take sides as well in the age-old problems of dog versus cat, bird versus bird, even bird versus worm. In my opinion, the State of Illinois and its local governing bodies already have enough to do without trying to control feline delinquency.

For these reasons, and not because I love birds the less or cats the more, I veto and withhold my approval from Senate Bill No. 93.

Assistant Secretary of the Navy H. Struve Hansel shakes hands with Stevenson on June 1, 1945, after presenting him with Navy's highest civilian award for services in World War II. Citation reads as follows:

CITATION

"For exceptional performance of outstanding service to the United States Navy as Special Assistant to the Secretary of the Navy from 30 June 1941 to 13 June 1944.

"During this most critical period of the Navy's greatest expansion, Mr. Stevenson rendered invaluable service to the entire Naval Establishment by ably assisting and counseling the Secretary of the Navy in the efficient operation of his office. Much credit is due Mr. Stevenson for his many suggestions and ideas which materially improved the organization and functioning of the Naval Establishment.

"By his keen understanding and intelligent appraisal of difficult problems, by his exercise of sound judgment and by his extreme devotion to duty, Mr. Stevenson has distinguished himself in a manner deserving of the Navy's highest civilian award."

/s/ JAMES FORRESTAL

Stevenson (right, holding glove) with Major John Boettiger (whose wife was FDR's daughter, Anna) and Lt. Commander Malcolm S. McLean (center) at San Pietro, Italy, in December, 1943. Town was still under fire from Germans at Cassino.

Stevenson with General Charles de Gaulle, French Ambassador to U. S., Henri Bonnet and Paul Miller, general manager of the Associated Press, at Washington reception for de Gaulle in 1945.

With naval officers, Stevenson inspected Canal Zone in 1942. During World War II, Stevenson inspected all theaters except China–Burma–India, covered almost 50,000 miles, mostly by air.

With Henry Wallace, then Vice-President, and Secretary of the Navy Frank Knox, Stevenson inspected Naval Air Station in August, 1943. Wallace and Knox, who died the next year, autographed this picture.

In 1941, Stevenson was practicing law in Chicago.

In 1945, he helped organize United Nations.

In 1942, Governor tried out Link trainer in Canal Zone. His caption for this scrap-book picture: "Waiting for the weather to clear."

At London in 1945, Stevenson chats with Ukrainian delegate Dr.
Manuilsky at meeting of U. N. Preparatory Commission.

At Lake Success in December, 1947, Stevenson talks with advisors to
United Kingdom delegation to second session of the U.N.

At October, 1946, meeting of U.N. General Assembly in New York, Stevenson sits with Warren Austin (left) and John Foster Dulles . . .

chats with lady delegate. . .

smokes while Gromyko holds forth . . .

studies while Gromyko listens . . .

listens to speech with Eleanor
Roosevelt (second from left) . . .

At January, 1946, meeting of General Assembly in London, Stevenson
talks to Secretary of State James F. Byrnes. At right is Senator Tom
Connally, behind him Postmaster General Frank C. Walker. Senator
Vandenberg talks to John Foster Dulles behind Stevenson.

Stevenson relaxes in Lake Forest
swimming pool (1939) . . .

plays golf with friends Robert Clark
and Edward K. Dunn at French
Lick, Indiana (1947) . . .

and goes for a sleigh ride, pulled by "Colonel" and pulling youngest son, John Fell.

3

In NOVEMBER *1951 Stevenson wrote* Korea in Perspective, *the lead article in the April 1952 issue of* Foreign Affairs. *Taken together with his Northwestern Founders' Day speech, this article makes up a fairly full definition of his views on the foreign problems currently confronting any candidate for national leadership. Appearing when it did,* Korea in Perspective *added to the influences then gathering to create the Stevenson presidential boom. However, while it received wide attention from the serious students of international matters who compose the bulk of the magazine's limited circulation, it was not addressed to, nor read by, the general public. Since the article now has a much wider importance than it had when it was written, due to the increased recognition of the author, it is reprinted here in full. In permitting it to be reprinted, Stevenson said:*

"Reprint it if you like, but I must admit it seems to me pretty wordy."

THE STRENGTH of America is rooted in a great principle — individuals are an end, not a means. That is the American idea. Schools, colleges, labor unions, political parties and the Government of the United States exist for American men

*Reprinted by permission from Foreign Affairs, April, 1952.

and women; never the other way round. The corollary of the idea is that every individual must take responsibility for the whole. He must himself take responsibility for the safety and the wise development of his country, and for the selection of policies which determine its safety and progress. The basic requirement for the success of a democratic system of this sort is, of course, that individuals see their country's problems whole. In a word, they must have perspective.

This is especially true, and especially difficult to achieve, in problems of foreign relations. "Foreign policy," in the year 1952, covers the globe. In no other area is it so easy to have a picture of many single trees and no idea what the forest looks like. But the neatest description of a tree is not a dependable map for making one's way through a forest.

Gaining perspective on American foreign policy begins with gaining a view of America's position in the world — her position as a World Power. This can be indicated in half a dozen words: American interests, power and responsibilities are world-wide. Alongside this must be set two other basic facts which are revealed in any full view of the field of foreign policy. One is that a world-wide imperialist war is now being carried on by the Soviet Union and its Communist satellites. The other is the existence of a world-wide organization of states "united in strength to maintain international peace and security" — the United Nations. The relationship of these three great world forces — the United States, the Soviet Union and the United Nations — are the primary elements in the American problem of foreign policy today.

There is no possibility of doubting (and no reason for ignoring!) the fact that the Soviet objective is one world — one Communist world. Thanks to the interconnections of Soviet imperialism and international revolutionary communism the Soviet Government is able always to pursue a dual strategy. The strategy is implicit in Bolshevik theory. From the day Lenin seized power in Russia — and indeed even earlier — his strategy was one of "double diplomacy:" a long-range policy, a short-range policy; a set of slogans for home consumption, a set of slogans for foreign confusion; warfare against the Russian people, warfare against all foreigners; political warfare and military warfare, simultaneous or interchangeable. No American foreign policy which does not allow for the over-all view of this Soviet duplicity, and which does not have both political and military weapons to counter it, can provide for our safety or enable us to carry out our responsibilities. The effort to achieve the over-all view is the basic task of Americans.

This is a campaign year in America, and we must expect over-simplification of issues and contradictory advice regarding them. Men, even responsible men, will wander far afield in search of votes. They will capitalize every discontent, every prejudice, every credulity, even in the deadly serious business of foreign policy. Will we emerge from the ordeal of the campaign more aware of the true causes of our difficulties and the magnitude of the stakes involved? Or less aware? Will we emerge better prepared to turn with fortitude to the work in hand? Or worse prepared? These are the central questions which should be answered decisively by the elections.

The election campaign has not begun too well in this respect. What, for example, are we to make of the repeated charge that the Korean was is "Truman's war," that the President thrust the United States into it lightly, inadvisedly and against the best interest of the Republic, that it is a "useless" war, and that "we stand exactly where we stood three years ago"? What is the purpose of the petulant animosity shown in some quarters toward the United Nations, and of the despairing conclusion in others that the United Nations has "let us down" and has become more a danger to us than a source of strength? This kind of talk is deplorable because it belittles the heroic sacrifices of American and Allied soldiers and depreciates the value of an international effort that cost us an even greater war to achieve. But it seems to me more than deplorable. It seems to me dangerously misleading. What are we to think of statesmen who don't lead, but who mislead?

The purpose of such utterances apparently is to seek to make a single individual responsible for developments resulting from past actions taken by all the American people. Our present troubles do not stem from the bad judgment or weakness of particular individuals, any more than it would be true to say that any one man's insight has been responsible for our successes — which have been notable. Our setbacks and our victories are alike the products of the full sweep of recent history; and for that we are all of us responsible. Twice within twenty-five years this country felt compelled to intervene in wars to redress the balance of power in the world. At the close of World II, with Britain exhausted and France demoralized, with German and Japanese power crushed, the United States and the Soviet Union stood virtually face to face, with other nations polarized around them. Imperial Russia, historically a great expanding Power, now heavily armed and equipped with the seductive weapon of revolutionary communism, soon showed that she was on the move again, seizing weaker nations here, probing there, pressing relentlessly with propaganda and infiltration against the free world. During the second world war, and with the experience of the prewar period fresh in their minds, our people concluded that isolation was no solution to the problem of security in a shrunken world. Their decision was reinforced by this rising spectre of another ruthless imperial power on the march. They concluded that the time to stop aggression, like a plague, was before it started; and that the way to do it was by organized community action.

It is now some time since we engaged in the formidable task of developing the community of free peoples — first through the United Nations, since the problem is inexorably world-wide; then through the North Atlantic Treaty Organization, designed to strengthen a particularly exposed salient — the Western European "peninsula" of the vast central "Heartland," as the great geographer Mackinder called it; simultaneously by strengthening the important Organization of American States in our own hemisphere; and by numerous other treaties and agencies. The American response to the North Korean aggression, which was supplied and equipped by the Soviet Union and could not have occurred without its instigation or approval, was therefore neither erratic nor impetuous. It was part and parcel of a strategy of collective security which had been in the making for a long time and which had been urged, welcomed and agreed upon long since with virtual unanimity by the American people.

When North Korean forces invaded the Republic of Korea on June 25, 1950, with the full support of Peking and Moscow, most of us knew what was at stake. One of the men who took part in the long, anxious meeting at Blair House gave the simplest explanation of the decision: "This attack on South Korea is like Hitler's reoccupation of the Rhineland." Historians have for years commented on the tragic mistake of France in not ordering the instant mobilization of the French Army when Hitler's troops started marching — and on the shortsightedness of the British and others who failed to urge and support such action.

An American columnist pointed out in June 1950 that President Truman's decision, taken with the virtually unanimous support of the American people and their representatives in Congress, recalled the words of former Secretary of State Henry L. Stimson following what he termed "the tragedy of timidity" in the Far Eastern crisis of the early thirties: "I broke out and said," wrote Mr. Stimson, "that I was living in a world where all my troubles came from the same thing . . . where we are constantly shut in by the timidity of governments . . . and I said that the time had come when somebody has got to show some guts."

Senator Knowland, Republican, of California, a frequent critic of Administration Far Eastern policy, was the first to take the floor of the Senate in support of the President's announcement: "I believe that, in this very important step the President of the United States has taken to uphold the hands of the United Nations and the free peoples of the world, he should have the overwhelming support of all Americans, regardless of their partisan affiliations." In similar vein the approving chorus swept the Congress and the country. One member of Congress only opposed American armed aid to the victims of Communist aggression — Representative Marcantonio of New York, subsequently defeated for re-election.

To call Korea "Truman's war" distorts the entire historical significance of our prompt response through the United Nations to the cynical Communist challenge to the whole concept of collective peace and security — the concept which we are pledged to defend and which only the Soviet Union has an interest in destroying. Mr. Truman happened to be the President of the United States when the challenge came. Did the American people wish it to go unanswered, did they wish all hope for the new community of nations banded together in strength to limit war to collapse? *Time* magazine, with a backward glance at the equivocation of the League of Nations, summed up the matter simply: "This time, when the challenge came, the United States accepted it." So did the United Nations. To call this "Truman's war" is to deny the manifest common approval of our prompt action.

Inevitably there are differences of opinion now about the course of events in Korea. The decision to defeat the challenge of aggression by force brought grievous losses in blood and treasure. The first feeling of relief which welcomed the stern, swift action of two years ago has given way to criticism and impatience. In taking stock of where we now stand, however, we should not talk about our problems out of context.

There is nothing to be gained by what General Marshall used to call "fighting the problem." The problem is that the Soviet rulers and their Communist satellites consider themselves at war with us, but that we are not in fact at war with them. It is complicated by the further fact that war in their sense is waged interchangeably by military and political instruments. In view of this it is proper for us to ask ourselves what would have happened if we had "fought the problem" — that is, evaded it — in June 1950. What would have happened if the United States and the United Nations had ignored the Korean aggression?

I can venture a guess. Our friends throughout Asia and in the Pacific would with perfect reason have doubted our intention to resist Soviet design elsewhere in that area, and they would of necessity have taken the path of appeasement. Disillusionment would also have swept Western Europe at this impressive demonstration of Soviet-satellite power and of American indecision in the face of a direct challenge. Then would not the Soviet Union having challenged us successfully in Korea, have followed that challenge with another? And still another? Munich would follow Munich. Our vacillation would have paralyzed our will and worked havoc in the community of like-minded nations. Then when we did succeed in pulling ourselves together we would have found it too late to organize a common front with our friends. I think there is good reason to believe that the resolute action by the United Nations forces in Korea not only gained time in the East but saved NATO in the West. The alternative was to surrender all positions of strength, to enfeeble if not destroy the grand alliance of the free — and then, perhaps, to resort in desperation to a general war when our moral, political and strategic position had been weakened disastrously.

There is, of course, no tidy solution to the Korean problem, precisely because it is only a part of the whole Soviet imperialist drive — an episode, really, in the sweep of history which relentlessly confronts freedom with thralldom. In a world where the objective of the Soviet Union is to eliminate every rival center of power we must measure our gains and our losses not in absolute terms but in relation to the over-all situation. The Soviet rulers themselves describe their struggle with the non-Soviet world as war. In Korea we have made plain to the Kremlin that we are not fooled by its use of catspaws, and that we recognize war fought at second hand when we see it. Our object is to convince them that other aggressions, disguised or direct, will meet the same response, and thus deter them from a perhaps fatal gamble. At the same time, by limiting the war in Korea, we hope to avoid a third general holocaust. We are trying to use force not only to frustrate our immediate antagonists in the hills of Korea but to preserve world peace. For that reason the full settlement of the Korean problem is likely to take a long time and to wait upon the settlement of many other issues. Once again, perspective.

It is possible, of course, that we may fail in our effort to keep the Korean fighting limited: for just as it takes only one to start a war, so it takes only one to prolong it. The aggressor is the one who decides whether or not the war he has started can be limited. But we have diligently and painfully sought to keep it from spreading. Given the terms of the problem, there is no guarantee of success. It simply seems wiser to pay large insurance premiums than to look forward to rebuilding after the fire.

Meanwhile, some of the positive gains of our policy thus far may properly be noted. Talk of the "uselessness" of the Korean war gained currency only when negotiations for an armistice dragged out, and after we had in fact accomplished the primary objective of stopping the aggression and driving the aggressors back from whence they came — across the 38th parallel. Assured of satisfactory armistice terms, we would have little purpose in continuing hostilities. But what sort of logic is it to say that because the continuation of the war does not serve our interests, the entire enterprise was futile from the start?

And while it is too early to make any final estimate of the Korean experience, it is also foolish and misleading to say we "stand exactly where we stood three years ago." The first reason is that the Korean engagement put the American rearmament effort into high gear. Having virtually obliterated our armed strength after World War II, we were slow to reconcile ourselves to the economic dislocation and sacrifices needed to recreate it. Proof that the Soviet Union would speed the advance of troops across a national frontier dissolved our reluctance. Now our increasing strength not only puts us in a better position to answer further military aggression. We also are in a position to conduct a bolder diplomacy — in other words, to take the initiative politically.

Second, our leadership in fighting aggression in Korea not only saved the moral and psychological defenses of Western Europe from possible disintegration but sparked the rapid build-up there of physical defenses. The demonstration that there could be successful resistance to the Soviet Union and imperial Communism gave the leaders of Europe hope and persuaded their peoples to accept more readily the burdens and risks of rearmament. It is routine politics for even the timid and faint of heart among us to talk about the necessity for American "leadership." Had America not in fact led, but shrunk from the challenge of Korea, would Europe have tackled the vast, costly and painful program of organizing Western defenses?

Third, the Soviet Union now knows that the path of conquest is mortally dangerous. The Korean aggression very likely was planned as merely the first of a series of military actions — initially by satellites, finally to be undertaken by the Soviet Union itself. If so, the lesson of Korea may be of historic importance. Speculation about possible adjustments in the thinking of the men in the Kremlin must be cautious. Perhaps for a time the Soviet Union will now content itself with manoeuvres in the cold war; or perhaps Western strength of will is to be further tested by some other military challenge; or perhaps Stalin and his partners will reason that a full-scale war (which Communist theory foreshadows) had best be waged in the immediate future rather than when the armament programs of the West become more fully effective. It can be argued that Stalin, in his old age, will never risk the loss of the empire he has built up; but it can also be said that he may believe what his sycophants tirelessly chant — that he is "the greatest commander of all times and peoples"*—and that if the "terrible collisions" prophesied in Communist dogma are indeed to come, then they had best come while he is still alive. We dare not tie our policies to any one assumption regarding Soviet intentions. Whatever those intentions are, however, the Soviet miscalculation in Korea will make them harder of fulfillment.

Fourth, our support of the first great collective military effort of the United Nations to resist aggression demonstrated that the organization is adaptable to the role of enforcement as well as that of conciliation. In the crisis there emerged proof of the viability of the concept of collective security, a fact of inestimable importance for the security of every free country — including our own. Sixteen countries contributed fighting forces. The policies of the free nations have been concerted consistently in the votes relating to Korea. While troops of the Republic of Korea and the United States have been obliged to carry the main burden of the fighting and we may properly regret the absence of more help from others, we should not overlook the fact that the responsibility for resistance to Communist military aggression in certain other areas is borne more by others than by ourselves. If another showdown is provoked elsewhere, the system of collective security is in better shape now to meet it than it was before June 1950. In short, while Korea has not proved definitively that collective security *will* work, it has prevented the Soviet Union from proving that it *won't* work. And the Korean experience, moreover, has hastened the development of the General Assembly of the United Nations

*Pravda, November 6, 1951.

as an agency of enforcement, free from the Soviet veto.

Fifthly, we may record that the successful resistance in Korea has contributed greatly to the successful negotiation of a Treaty of Peace with Japan, as well as of arrangements satisfactory to us regarding the future security of that country. A failure on our part to give evidence of a willingness to act in a time of crisis would not have encouraged the Philippines, Australia, New Zealand and Japan to enter into the recently negotiated network of the Pacific security treaties.

One further national advantage from this "useless" war deserves at least to be mentioned. We have learned vital military lessons in Korea. I am not competent to discuss improvements in tactics and weapons, nor would it be appropriate here to do so. But a more effective use of forces and armaments as a result of long testing under actual combat conditions is to be counted as an important residual return on our investment in this savage conflict.

So much for this historic frustration of Communist military conquest. Soviet policy, however, is dual. Indispensable as was the United Nations for the repulse of the aggression in Korea, it is needed even more in the political struggle in which we are engaged.

Obviously the United Nations has not fulfilled all the high hopes that some people entertained when it was founded. The idea that it would automatically usher in an era of sweetness and light was exaggerated at the start, as was soon demonstrated when Soviet imperialism made plain that it was determined to prevent the organization of the world on any but its own terms. But again look at the woods, not the trees. Although the United Nations has worked haltingly, at times badly — it has worked. Since the present *world-wide* coalition of free peoples is inconceivable without a central forum and instrument for discussion and adjustment, it remains an indispensable part of our foreign policy. The problem is to make the organization function more perfectly. Granted that it has done little to adjust the differences between the Soviets and the free world: so long as the Soviet rulers prosecute their dual war — against their own people and against all outsiders — there is no reason to expect that it will. Even so, it maintains at least formal contact between the two worlds. Our willingness to keep the door open for talk and negotiation is essential evidence for our friends (who stand more deeply in the shadow of the Russian fist than we do) that we will accept any reasonable opportunity to better relations and avoid all-out war.

Again, the United Nations is indispensable as an agency for concerting policies among the free states, including (as we found in the case of Korea) enforcement action. The bulk of the members of the General Assembly are free nations. In spite of the discouraging and frustrating debate with the Russians — or perhaps thanks in part to their recalcitrant and dogmatic postures — policies have been developed in the General Assembly to cope better with many of the perils to economic stability and international justice. Obviously not all international questions need or should be put before the United Nations; and certainly we should use our influence to preserve a safe boundary line between those domestic affairs which are our own concern and the external affairs which are of concern to all. These are matters for careful study and progress by stages. But surely to prevent a trespass it is not sensible to shoot the watchman; nor to burn down the barn to roast a pig.

The audible yearning to escape from it all, the murmurs and cries of disdain for the "meddlers," the "globalists" and the "foreigners" now sometimes heard in our midst, are strangely familiar. Are they groans from the ghost of America First, still looking for an unassailable Gibraltar, safe from assault by men — or ideas? I doubt if many Americans will be drawn into a renewal of that wishful search. I think the eagle, not the ostrich, will continue to be the American emblem.

The reality of the matter is that American power is going to be preponderant on our side of the Iron Curtain for many years to come, and that without this concentration of power there would be no possibility of pulling the free world together or providing for an effective common defense. Our friends abroad know this. And the reality is likewise that a successful military defense, and a successful political advance, depend on the cooperation of a large number of governments — in the Far East and the Middle East, in Europe and in this hemisphere. More, our ability to take the initiative depends not simply on the cooperation of governments, but on the good will of peoples who support these governments. We live in a new world — a world where the stronger need the help of the weaker!

We should not be too surprised that the same nations that formerly were alarmed at our isolationism are now concerned about how we will use our power. Just because of our strength we are a target for much unjust resentment. Surely we can call upon a sufficiently long historical perspective, and a sufficiently intelligent understanding of human nature, not to be too much surprised by that. Men in lands which have recently freed themselves from old tyrannies know all too well the temptations of power. Their fear that we may fall into old errors is not unnatural. And indeed, who among us would dare say that we do not have much to learn? No single nation, viewing the world from a particular perspective, can have a monopoly of insight. We must take the criticisms as they come — sometimes as fair warning — and redouble our efforts to develop mutual policies based on adequate understanding between sovereign but interdependent partners.

Sovereign international authorities over a wide area, or fully unified political councils in the whole of the free world, are not in prospect. We must concert our policies with those of our friends by the instruments available. Our aim should be to improve the machinery for mutual give and take, both in the United Nations and in regional agencies. Fortunately, the menace of the Soviet Union tends to promote a common view among those marked out as prey; and it can further be said that despite differences in approach and emphasis, much of the free world now shares a wide range of political and economic interests which move it in the direction of unity. The United Nations is an invaluable instrument for harmonizing differences in those interests. It and other agencies such as the North Atlantic Treaty Organization have given us — and our friends — considerable experience in this unceasing task of mutual accommodation. The United States will find support among peoples in the free states to the degree that they believe that we do not simply consult our own interests but give consideration to their interests as well — that we in truth have a "decent respect for the opinions of mankind." Other nations have a reciprocal obligation to give weight to our interests too. There is no doubt that our power gives us an advantage in this process. But neither is there room to doubt that if we wish allies who will go forward with us with courage and fortitude into the risks of the future, they must be willing and confident allies.

Let us also remember that the alternative to the United Nations is not a vacuum. There would at once be formed another "world organization." The Soviet Union, true to its policy of duplicity, has this alternative organization already in hand — presumably to be based on the "World Peace Council," formed on November 22, 1950, at the "Second World Peace Conference" in Warsaw, Professor Frederic Joliot (known better as Joliot-Curie through his appropriation of a revered name on which he has no claim of blood) presided, as "President of the Bureau," at the most recent meeting, in Vienna last November. Various trained seals were brought from all corners of the world. For the gist of the program one can take almost any of the old Marxist fighting slogans and substitute the word "peace" for the word "revolution." In Soviet double-talk they mean the same.

The burden of my argument, then, based on the meaning of our experience in Korea as I see it, is that we have made historic progress toward the establishment of a viable system of collective security. To deprecate our large and decisive share in that undertaking as "useless" is both mischievous and regressive. It will stiffen no backs, lift no hearts and encourage no one except our enemies.

The particulars of the forward political movement which our successful acceptance of the Soviet challenge in Korea has made possible for us would form the beginnings of a new analysis, not a conclusion for this one. What is incontrovertible, I think, is that America needs and wants allies. I think most Americans know this. I think we believe that the redress in the balance of power in the world must be completed, and quickly. I think we believe that the great experiment in collective security on which we embarked in 1945 is still in the long run our best chance for peace. I think we believe that international cooperation is more than elocution. In short, I think most of us have convictions about the position of the United States in the world today and accept the risks and responsibilities inherent in that position. The nature of the American decision was shown — is shown — in Korea. Shall we retreat from that decision? Shall we go it alone? Or shall we go forward with allies? When our experience in Korea has been placed in perspective, this remains the issue behind the dust and turmoil of this election year.

4

GOVERNOR STEVENSON'S *relations with Alger Hiss have been the subject of considerable controversy. Most of this centers around a deposition from the Governor which was introduced as evidence into the first Hiss trial, which resulted in a hung jury. The impression created by the Governor's political opponents has been that the deposition represented an attempt by Stevenson to whitewash the defendant's character. The Governor and his supporters have contended that on the contrary it merely set forth information about what other people thought about Hiss, and that it in no way even implied any opinion on Stevenson's part as to the defendant's character, let alone his guilt or innocence. It is hard to appraise the merits of this argument without scrutinizing the deposition itself, which was taken in the Governor's office in Springfield and reads as follows:*

IN THE UNITED STATES DISTRICT COURT
FOR THE SOUTHERN DISTRICT OF NEW YORK

United States of America		
against	}	C-128-402
ALGER HISS,		
Defendant.		

Deposition of Honorable Adlai Stevenson, Governor of the State of Illinois, before William B. Chittenden, United

ADLAI E. STEVENSON

States Commissioner in and for the Southern District of Illinois, taken at Springfield, Illinois, on June 2, 1949.

PRESENT:
William B. Chittenden, United States Commissioner, Springfield, Illinois
HON. ADLAI STEVENSON, Governor of the State of Illinois
Harry L. Livingstone, *Reporter.*

MR. CHITTENDEN: Governor Stevenson, the purpose of this hearing is to take your deposition on written direct interrogatories in behalf of the Defendant Alger Hiss in a case entitled United States of America against Alger Hiss, Defendant, now pending in the United States District Court for the Southern District of New York, and upon written cross-interrogatories in behalf of the United States of America, the complainant in said cause; *pursuant to an order of the United States District Court for the Southern District of New York, entered on May 24, 1949,* a certified copy of which order I now exhibit to you.

Will you please therefore stand, raise your right hand, and be sworn.

"Do you, Adlai E. Stevenson, also known as Adlai Ewing Stevenson, solemnly swear that the testimony which you are about to give upon written direct and cross interrogatories in the above mentioned case of United States v. Alger Hiss, Defendant, will be the truth, the whole truth and nothing but the truth, so help you God?"

GOVERNOR STEVENSON: I do.

DIRECT INTERROGATORIES IN BEHALF
OF DEFENDANT ALGER HISS

Q. No. 1. State your name and address.
A. No. 1. Adlai E. Stevenson, Executive Mansion,
Springfield, Illinois.
*Q. No. 2. What is your official position at the present
time?*
A. No. 2. Governor of Illinois.
*Q. No. 3. State the official positions which you have held
in the past.*
A. No. 3. I was special counsel to the Agricultural
Adjustment Administration, Washington, June, 1933 to January, 1934. I was assistant general counsel of the Federal
Alcohol Control Administration, Washington, January, 1934
to September, 1934. I was special assistant to the Secretary
of the Navy, Washington, from July, 1941 to June, 1944.
I was special assistant to the Secretary of State from February,
1945 to August, 1945. I was United States Minister in
London, September, 1945 to March, 1946. I was United
States representative to the Preparatory Commission of the
United Nations, London, September, 1945 to January, 1946.
I was senior adviser to the United States Delegation to the
General Assembly of the United Nations, first session, London, January-February, 1946. I was alternate United States
Delegate to the General Assembly of the United Nations,
New York, September, 1946 to November, 1946. I was
alternate United States Delegate to the General Assembly of
the United Nations, New York, September, 1947 to November, 1947. I think that is all.

ADLAI E. STEVENSON

Q. No. 4. How long have you known Mr. Alger Hiss, the defendant?

A. No. 4. Since June or July, 1933.

Q. No. 5. Where, when and under what circumstances did you first become acquainted with him?

A. No. 5. We served together in the Legal Division of the Agricultural Adjustment Administration in Washington in 1933.

Q. No. 6. State the nature and extent of your association with him from that time until the present.

A. No. 6. In the Agricultural Adjustment Administration in 1933 we were working on different commodities. Our contact was frequent but not close nor daily. I had no further contact with him until I met him again in the State Department when I went to work there in 1945. Upon my arrival in the State Department at the end of February or early March to the end of April, when Mr. Hiss left for the San Francisco conference, he was, I think, largely preoccupied with the arrangements for that conference, for the United Nations conference on international organization at San Francisco. During that interval, from the first of March to the end of April, I was engaged in other matters and met him mostly in intra-departmental meetings and in connection with some aspects of the plan for the San Francisco conference, largely relating to matters pertaining to the handling of the press at the conference. I was at the conference, myself, as assistant to the Secretary of State from about the 10th of May until the end of June. During that interval Mr. Hiss was Secretary General of the conference and I was attached to the United States Delegation. Our paths did not cross in a business way but we met occasionally at official social functions.

Back in Washington during July, I had some conferences with him in connection with preparations for the presentation of the United Nations charter to the Senate for ratification.

I resigned from the Department early in August, 1945, and so far as I recall I did not meet Mr. Hiss personally again until he came to London in January, 1946, with the United States Delegation to the First General Assembly of the United Nations. During that conference in January and February we had offices nearby each other and met frequently at delegation meetings and staff conferences.

I returned to the United States in March, 1946 and I do not believe I met Mr. Hiss again until the United Nations General Assembly in New York in 1947. At that time he was connected with the Carnegie Endowment for International Peace and I visited with him on one or two occasions at my office in the United States Delegation Headquarters in connection with the budget for the United Nations, which was one of my responsibilities as a member of the American Delegation. I have not seen him since.

Q. No. 7. *Have you known other persons who have known Mr. Alger Hiss?*

A. No. 7. Yes.

Q. No. 8. *From the speech of those persons, can you state what the reputation of Alger Hiss is for integrity, loyalty and veracity?*

A. No. 8. Yes.

Q. No. 9. (a) *Specify whether his reputation for integrity is good or bad?*

ADLAI E. STEVENSON

A. No. 9. (a) Good.

Q. No. 9. (b) Specify whether his reputation for loy alty is good or bad?

A. No. 9. (b) Good.

Q. No. 9. (c) Specify whether his reputation for veracity is good or bad?

A. No. 9. (c) Good.

* * * * * * * * * *

CROSS INTERROGATORIES IN BEHALF OF UNITED STATES OF AMERICA, COMPLAINANT IN SAID CAUSE

Q. No. 1. Were you ever a guest in the home of defendant Alger Hiss at any time in 1935, to and including 1938?

A. No. 1. No, I have never been a guest in Mr. Hiss' home.

Q. No. 3.* Did you, prior to 1948, hear that the defendant Alger Hiss during the years 1937 and 1938 removed confidential and secret documents from the State Department and made such documents available to persons not authorized to see or receive them?

A. No. 3. No.

Q. No. 4. Did you, prior to 1948, hear reports that the defendant Alger Hiss was a Communist?

A. No. 4. No.

Q. No. 5. Did you, prior to 1948, hear reports that the defendant Alger Hiss was a Communist sympathizer?

*There is no Question No. 2 owing to an error in counting made by the Court stenographer.

A. No. 5. No.

Q. No. 6. State whether or not you ever attended Harvard College or Harvard Law School?

A. No. 6. Harvard Law School, September, 1922 to June, 1924.

Q. No. 7. State whether or not you ever attended Princeton University?

A. No. 7. Yes, September, 1918 to June, 1922

I, Adlai E. Stevenson, do hereby certify that the foregoing questions were put to me by William B. Chittenden, United States Commissioner for the Southern District of Illinois, and the foregoing answers were made by me; that my testimony, after being fully transcribed, was submitted to me for examination, and has been read by me and such changes therein as I have desired have been entered upon the said deposition by the said William B. Chittenden, with a statement of the reasons given by me for making the same; in witness whereof, I hereunto subscribe my name this 2nd day of June, 1949.

Stevenson was recently asked how well he had in fact known Hiss and how the matter of the deposition had come up. Stevenson said:

To answer the second question first, it came up because, when I was asked by Hiss's lawyers to testify as to Hiss's reputation, I agreed to answer any questions as best I could but declined to go to New York. It seems to me that it will be a very sad day for Anglo Saxon justice when any man, and especially a lawyer, will refuse to give honest evidence in a criminal trial for fear the defendant in an action may eventually be found guilty. What would happen to our whole system of law if such timidity prevailed? I feel very strongly that it is one of the basic responsibilities of any citizen, and most especially of lawyers, to testify to the best of their ability on any case in which they may have evidence that either side considers relevant. As to the value of their testimony, that is for the jury to decide.

In this Hiss case, I just can't imagine what people would have expected me to do. Was I supposed to say that I didn't know Hiss, when I most certainly did know him? Was I supposed to say that his reputation was bad? Obviously it was good, or he wouldn't have held the exalted public position he was in when I met him in the State Department in 1945. Nor would he have been selected as President of the Carnegie Endowment by some of the most conservative and respected businessmen in the country. The only basis I can see for finding fault with my deposition would be on the assumption that I lied because I was supposed to have some confidential information about his activities eight or ten years before. I had not seen or even heard of him from 1933 to 1945 and when I did meet him again I never heard even a syllable of suspicion about him. I must admit, this talk about that deposition irks me a good deal. If I were asked to answer the same questions tomorrow, in all honesty I would have to give exactly the same answers; and also I would have just as little cause to quarrel with the final verdict of the court.

It was suggested that possibly some of the confusion caused by the deposition arose because Hiss had based his defense upon the premise that his reputation was so good that it placed him above suspicion; and that this misuse of reputation by the defendant unavoidably cast doubt upon the motives of witnesses who testified to its excellence. The Governor considered this possibility and said:

Well, there may be something to that; it might explain part of the reaction to what I said. Now, you ask me how well I knew Hiss, and I'll tell you. I met him first when I went to Washington in 1933 but I saw very little of him in the AAA. We were working on different things. I spent most of my time in California and out of town working on marketing agreements for special crops, fruit and so forth. I don't remember even seeing him again until 1945 when I went to work in the State Department a month or so before the San Francisco conference. He came up to me one day and said: "I'm Alger Hiss. We used to work together in the AAA." I remember feeling surprised, that he remembered me.

I saw very little of him in San Francisco; I was up at the Fairmount Hotel at our delegation office most of the time and he was down town at the headquarters of the international secretariat of which he was the chief. Back in Washington in July we conferred occasionally about the Senate hearings on ratification of the charter. But I left very soon to return to Chicago. I saw quite a lot of him the next winter in London during the six weeks of the assembly meeting and met him again a few times in New York in 1947, when he was President of the Carnegie Foundation. I never did know him well; I never went to his house; I never met his wife. If I had been asked about his character, my opinion would have been superficial. But that wasn't what was asked. I ran into many people who knew him well and had worked with him extensively; I was asked what they thought of him. I told the truth about that to the best of my ability because they all seemed to regard him very highly.

5

Dᴜʀɪɴɢ ᴛʜᴇ ᴘᴇᴀᴋ *of the Stevenson presidential boom, Stevenson said:*

"I have been asked more questions than the Quiz kids and Mr. Anthony put together."

Herewith some of the questions the Governor has been asked along with his answers:

From U. S. News and World Report*

Q. You have said publicly, Governor, that you were not a candidate for the Democratic presidential nomination. Is this a firm decision on your part?

A. It most assuredly is. On January 5th last, after the most prolonged and earnest consideration, I announced that I was a candidate for re-election as Governor of Illinois. That is what I have been ever since that announcement, and what I am now. I do not see how it is possible to be a candidate for two different offices at the same time. I am not that, nor will I ever be. . . .

Q. What is your principal reason for not wishing to be a candidate for the presidential nomination?

*Reprinted from U. S. News & World Report, an independent weekly news magazine published at Washington, D.C. Copyright 1952 United States News Publishing Corporation.

ADLAI E. STEVENSON

A. I believe I have indicated it already in my first answer. If I had wanted to be a candidate for the nomination as President, I would not have announced my candidacy for renomination as Governor. I do not believe that it is either morally or practically possible to be a simultaneous candidate for both.

There are, of course, other considerations which only serve to buttress this conclusion. I have been a resident of Illinois all my life, and my family roots here go back over a hundred years. I am genuinely interested in what happens in — and to — the State of Illinois. I have become deeply engrossed in my work as Governor, and I have invested in it all of my time and energy for over three years. I sincerely believe that the full fruits of that investment, in terms of better government in Illinois, are still to be gathered, and I would like to have a hand in that harvest.

I, and the many fine people whom I have induced to help me in this job, have a lot of unfinished business. For me that is a more than adequate reason for not aspiring to any other office, however exalted.

Q. *But since you want to be the Democratic candidate for Governor this year, is it not essential to your party's success in Illinois that there be a strong national ticket?*

A. I have no crystal ball to tell me at this time who will head the Democratic party's national ticket, but I am confident that that ticket will be a strong one. I have the same confidence that we are going to win in Illinois because I think that the majority of our citizens like what we have been trying to do since 1949.

I do not underestimate the effect of a national campaign

on the election of State officers, but neither do I underestimate the large and increasing capacity of the voters to disentangle State from national issues and to mark their ballots accordingly. Most of the issues relating to the conduct of the business of the State of Illinois bear no relation to the issues which divide the parties nationally — and I expect that most people will vote for or against me on the basis of the former.

Q. In order to get a strong national ticket, isn't it important also to have a strong national platform, one that will attract a majority of the voters of your state?

A. The strength of the Democratic party nationally for the past several years has not, in my opinion, been due just to strong personalities on the national ticket. It has been due in a very substantial degree to the strength of the principles which the party has offered to the nation in its platform. I do not think that 1952 is going to be different from any of these preceding campaign years, and I am sure that both platform and ticket will be strong.

Q. What do you think are the essential points that ought to be stressed by the Democratic party in connection with international affairs?

A. The basic point, it seems to me, is that the hard fact of Soviet Communist imperialism presents a real danger to the free world now and for an indeterminate period to come. From this one fact flow many difficulties which we must face with understanding and stout hearts. The Democratic Party should continue to stress in the future, as it has in the past, the necessity for mobilizing our strength, both military and economic in support of the free nations of the world; the importance of continued working toward the international organization and maintenance of peace through the United Nations; the value of regional organizations of strength, such as NATO, the Latin-American Defense Treaty, and our new treaty arrangements in the Pacific; and the stepping up of the kind of technical help provided under the Point Four program.

I think that the Democratic party would be well advised to increase the emphasis on this last point and the whole approach which it represents. We cannot buy peace with dollars alone, if for no other reason than we do not have enough dollars; but we can preserve, and indeed enlarge the friendly area by lending the aid of our vast technological knowledge to millions of desperately poor people, who can only find their way to free political institutions through betterment in their material conditions.

Q. What is your opinion as to the feeling of the country to Republican policy on international affairs?

A. I do not believe that your question can be fairly answered without some specification as to which Republican policy on international affairs you are referring to. I am sure that many Republicans, and many Republican candidates, approve an international policy not essentially dissimilar to the Democratic policy of assistance to our friends and resistance to our foes. Indeed, most, if not all, of the points in that policy were originally constructed with Republican help. There are, of course, Republicans who appear to have quite a different policy on international affairs and, relating your question to them, I happen to think that the majority feeling of the country is against them.

Q. What do you think would be the impression outside

[188]

of the United States if a Republican, for example, like Taft were nominated?

A. If Senator Taft were to be nominated, I think that there would inevitably be grave apprehension in many responsible quarters of the free world over the possibility of his election. His voting record with respect to the organization of the strength of the free world could have no other result. I would like to make clear, however, that I do not believe American elections should be determined by opinion outside of the United States. It is enough for me that Senator Taft's voting record on international matters is fraught with what, I regard as grave peril to the future of the United States itself, and I would not expect that the American voter would be swayed by any other than this legitimate concern.

Q. What do you think would be the impression if a Republican like Eisenhower were nominated?

A. I do not see how General Eisenhower's nomination could be anything other than reassuring in foreign quarters, at least in the key area of Western Europe. The General's patently genuine devotion to the principle of building up the strength of Western Europe to resist aggression and his services in the pursuit of that objective have won him the good will of everybody in Europe, except perhaps the Communists.

Q. What do you think is the difference between the foreign policy that the Democratic Party will champion and the foreign policy that will probably come out of the Republican platform?

A. I do not think it possible to say at this time what foreign policy will be embodied in the Republican platform. That depends too much on the present struggle which is going on within the party. Contrarily, no matter who the Democratic nominee is, it seems clear that the party platform will champion the things to which I have already referred. I would hope, of course, that the Republican platform would bear a reasonably close resemblance to it because I believe in the bipartisan approach to foreign policy, especially in these critical times.

Q. Do you think that the Democratic Party will by its platform approve everything that has been done by the Truman Administration in foreign policy?

A. I should expect that the Democratic platform will re-affirm every basic position on foreign policy taken by the Truman Administration. Again, there may be room for variance as to detail, but, inasmuch as party platforms of necessity can deal only with basic principles, I do not anticipate that the platform will fail in any respect to approve these major points.

Q. Do you think that there have been some mistakes made in the Administration's foreign policy? Would you favor acknowledging them?

A. I always favor acknowledging mistakes when it has become clear that they have been made, and this applies to foreign policy as to everything else. This is the principle on which my administration has been conducted in Illinois, and I think that it has been popular. Certainly it is right.

To the extent that there have been mistakes in the Administration's foreign policy, I think they are in substantial part a result of our own zeal to build a peaceful world founded upon international trust and good will. We tried, perhaps too hard, at the close of the war and shortly thereafter, to work together in mutual amity with all of our major allies in World War II. We leaned over backwards to demonstrate our desire to secure the peace of the world through international cooperation.

Take our withdrawal from Korea, for example. We made a bargain which we carried out and which we expected Russia to carry out. Had there been good faith on both sides instead of only on one, that withdrawal presumably would not have been what it now appears to be, namely, a "mistake in the Administration's foreign policy." I also recall that it was a "mistake" which was popular throughout the length and breadth of the country at a time when all of us wanted to get the boys home from abroad and to rid ourselves as fast as possible of our military preoccupations after four years of war.

Q. Do you think that some of these mistakes were due to developments or circumstances beyond the control of anybody in this country?

A. As I have just indicated, I think that our "mistakes" are due to our hope that Russia would prove sincere about peace and international live and let live. That she has not been is the great and abiding misfortune of the world.

Q. Do you feel that the American Government should be committed against admission of Red China into the United Nations?

A. I am opposed to the admission of Red China into the United Nations. I do not see why this Government should enlarge the sphere of operation of any other government which has waged, and is waging, war against it and against the United Nations in defiance of all that the United Nations stands for. Since that is an amply sufficient reason for opposing the admission of Red China, I regard it as a waste of time to speculate about a lot of hypothetical contingencies.

Q. Do you think, if the Korean problem is not solved by the time the campaign ends, that public opinion would sanction stronger measures, especially in the event a truce were broken?

A. I hope that public opinion, without reference to the period of the campaign or any other event, will continue to maintain the resolute patience and wisdom about the Korean problem which it has exhibited in the main thus far. The prolonged truce negotiations in Korea, and the stalling and double-dealing which have characterized the Communist participation in them, surely is one of the most exasperating experiences to which the American public has ever been subjected.

It is always necessary to keep clear, however, what our objectives are in the Korean intervention and not to be stampeded into a new set of objectives which might well mean heavier involvement in war in the Far East. I think that the Communist tactics in Korea have been designed to bring about just such a shift. Fortunately, we have not fallen as yet into that trap, and I hope and pray that we never will. . . .

Q. Do you favor the maintenance of large American forces in Europe indefinitely, or do you think there should be a program of gradual withdrawal?

A. I believe in the maintenance in Europe of American forces for the period of time required to assure the protection of Europe. I recognize that the size of our forces there must always be limited by what is possible for us to do. The necessity of a large and increasing participation by the European countries themselves in this effort is manifest. I see no reason why, if the nations of Western Europe can attain a sufficient degree of economic strength and stability, they should not ultimately provide all the ground forces necessary for their security. To say now just when and how American ground forces are to be withdrawn would seem to me both impossible and unwise.

Q. How far should American man power be used in Asia and Europe?

A. As I have just said, I believe in using American man power in both Europe and Asia, within the limits of our capacity to do so, to the extent required to blunt the drives of Soviet imperialism. I reaffirm my conviction that, if we can create sufficient economic strength in both Asia and Europe, we can progressively reduce our man-power commitments in those areas. I can envision little but disaster, however, in committing American man power to hostilities in the morass of the China mainland.

Q. Do you believe that all international action by the United States should be governed by regional pacts like the North Atlantic Treaty and the Pacific Pact, or do you think there are circumstances in which the United States may have to go it alone?

A. The regional pacts are certainly most hopeful instruments of policy and action for the future. They have the advantage of pooling material strength and clarifying common ideals. It is conceivable, of course, that there may arise peculiar circumstances in which the United States will find itself confronted with a problem in an area where no regional pact exists. Without being able to anticipate the exact outlines of such a problem, I would say that I would not as a matter of principle require allies in every case as a condition precedent to action by this country. The defense of freedom can often be a lonely job, but it is not one which is to be evaded for that reason. I recall one nation, led by one magnificent individual, which was not afraid to stand up to aggression alone in recent time; and a great part of the globe, including ourselves, will be forever in their debt.

Q. Would the Democratic party in your judgement be well advised to adopt a civil-rights program with a compulsory Fair Employment Practices Commission?

A. I think that I can discuss the question of FEPC in the most meaningful terms if I relate it closely to my experience in Illinois. I have twice proposed to the Illinois Legislature the enactment of a fair-employment-practices law which contained machinery for petitioning for court enforcement of the commission's orders. We have accomplished a great deal toward the elimination of employment discrimination in Illinois recently through voluntary methods. But it seems to me that what we still need to assure to everyone in the state his fundamental right to earn his living free from the handicap of racial or religious discrimination is a Fair Employment Practices Commission with power to investigate complaints, to promote educational programs, to conciliate conflicts whereever possible, and, where efforts at voluntary adjustment fail, to seek the intervention of the judicial power in proper instances.

Now, what is good for Illinois may not, perhaps, be good for every other State; and this is the principal reason why I have hoped that the States individually would seek their own solutions of this like many other problems. There may be significant variances in conditions from state to state which warrant different approaches, and I have always believed that the states should be encouraged to function as experimental laboratories working for the best solutions of common problems. However, I regard the right to earn one's living free from discrimination founded on race, color and religion as so fundamental a part of the heritage of all our citizens that the failure of the States to solve the problem clearly warrants a federal approach.

As to the Democratic party program, I think the party cannot retreat from the platform plank adopted at the 1948 convention.

Q. What is your opinion of the so-called voluntary or educational plan to bring about the end of race discrimination in the economic field?

A. We should never become so preoccupied with the issue of compulsory powers for fair-employment commissions that we neglect continuous and persistent effort to eliminate racial discrimination on a voluntary basis. The voluntary way is always the best and cheapest way if it works. I certainly do not regard the two approaches as conflicting. They are and should always be complementary and coexistent. Indeed, in Illinois I think it fair to say that the mere presence on the legislative horizon of a Fair Employment Practices Commission has accelerated the tempo of the voluntary approach.

In my state, the Illinois State Chamber of Commerce,

which has steadfastly opposed my FEPC bills, has been doing a conscientious, intelligent and effective job in the educational field. Should my bill ever pass, I would hope and expect that that effort would still go on. The state would then be free to deal with the small percentage of inevitable chiselers who are not amenable to these voluntary efforts, and the great and overwhelming percentage of decent employers would continue to react affirmatively, as they have heretofore, to the educational approach.

Q. Have you had any exprience with state problems in connection with race segregation? How have you handled them?

A. We have had in Illinois during the last three years a few incidents created by the segregation problem. The most notorious, of course, was the so-called Cicero riot, which was set off by the effort of a colored family to move into an apartment house in a suburb of Chicago. The failure of the local law-enforcement officials to control that situation properly in time resulted in an ugly manifestation of violence which prompted me to send in the National Guard to restore order.

I have always felt that the overriding issue, at least for me as Governor, in any incident of this kind is the simple one of insistence upon observance of law and order. I will not countenance rioting, the destruction of property, and the rough handling of individuals, no matter what the cause and no matter what the character of the passions aroused. In this view, disorders provoked by racial troubles are no different from disorders provoked by any other cause.

I have observed the same principle in some of the restlessness occasioned by the breaking down of segregation in our public schools and, by and large, we have made encouraging progress in this area with a minimum of difficulty. This is not to say that we are out of the woods yet, or that the job is finished — and, indeed, only a few weeks ago we had a discouraging setback in Cairo, Ill. However, the force of the state power was again thrown behind the basic principle I have mentioned, and I think that we are again pointed in the right direction.

Q. Are you in favor of a repeal of the Taft-Hartley Act or do you think that the Democratic platform should favor modifications in the Act?

A. I am this much of an expert on the Taft-Hartley law: I know that any one who says flatly that he is either for or against that law is indulging our common weakness for oversimplification. The law comprises over 100 sections, and it deals with a vast and varying range of matters affecting labor relations. If those issues are considered one by one, as they must be, I do not believe that there is any single representative group of people who will be unanimous in their views on all.

That is certainly the way I feel about it. Some features of the law seem to me to advance the cause of good labor relations, and other features, in my opinion, do not. I could not conscientiously subscribe to any position with respect to the Taft-Hartley law which does not take account of its great variety, and I happen to think that most of the people of the country, including the unions, have come to realize that the Taft-Hartley law cannot be dealt with in such simple and absolute terms. Obviously you do not have the space for me to get into an extended discussion of these multiple issues. I think the Democratic platform should recommend modification.

Q. How far should government go in what is often called intervention in the economic life of the country?

A. No farther than is absolutely required by the necessities of the particular case. And such intervention as does occur should be primarily addressed to the maintenance and enforcement of competition in our economic life, not its destruction.

Q. Do you feel that the intervention should be confined primarily to emergencies, or do you think that there are certain areas of action which are now "affected with a public interest"?

A. That question does not mean much to me apart from specific cases. For example, I suppose that regulation of the rates and services of public utilities could be taken as an example of intervention by government in economic affairs. But those businesses have, for many years, been accepted as 'affected with a public interest" in both legal and practical terms, and I believe in sound and strong public regulation of them. Government ownership and operation of public-utility properties is, however, another instance of what might be comprehended within the concept of government intervention in economic life. I certainly would hope that intervention of this latter kind would be confined strictly to those cases where there is a need which is not and cannot be met by private capital.

I do not believe that government, whether federal, state or local, should take on any job which it is not absolutely required to do by the facts of the case. I have said repeatedly that I believe in government being as small in scope and as local in character as possible: and certainly that objective cannot be achieved were government is steadily enlarging its business ownership and management commitments.

Q. What is your opinion about the farm program of the Administration? Should it be modified, or do you think the platform should advocate its continuance?

A. If one of the principal objectives of a farm program is to assure to the farmers themselves a fair and reasonable measure of prosperity, then the present program must be working all right because, at least in my section of the country, the farmers generally seem to be in good shape. Any Government subsidy program should be constantly re-evaluated to determine if it serves the purpose for which it was intended and whether the need continues to exist.

The kind of farm problems with which I've been concerned for the last three years have to do with such purely local matters as the improvement of rural roads, enhancing the marketability of Illinois farm products, and putting on our big annual farm show — the state fair — at a reduced cost to the taxpayers. These state government agricultural problems, though important and intricate and demanding in themselves, are far off the main channel of the federal farm program. I have not neglected them to spend my time thinking about possible improvements in federal programs.

Q. Do you think that there is a considerable area in which federal expenses can be cut without endangering our military program?

A. No one can say whether budgets can be wisely cut without digging into them. I have not done this on the federal budget, and therefore I cannot speak with the authority which attaches to the words of my friend, Paul Douglas, who has done so. Perhaps I can best answer your question by saying that it has been my lot as Governor of Illinois to prepare and submit to the Legislature two executive budgets. The one I submitted in 1951, after the outbreak of the Korean War, was smaller than the one I submitted in 1949, a few months after I was first inaugurated.

I like to think that I was able to accomplish this, despite the inflationary trend, simply because in the interval I had learned much more about the intricacies of State government and scrutinized very closely the budget requests of the agencies under me. Anyway, that has made me believe, rightly or wrongly, that there is always fat to be found in governmental budgets, as in business or personal budgets, if one only has the time and energy to find it and the guts to eliminate it. Maybe I can answer your question even better by saying that I believe the State of Illinois would still be functioning if my second budget had been even smaller.

Q. Do you think that the expenditures on new proposals for social welfare should be eliminated entirely in a national emergency?

A. No. I think that proposals in this field should be much more carefully tested in an emergency period, to make sure that we are devoting our limited resources to matters of the highest priority. But I do not believe that it is possible flatly to say that all progress in social improvement must of necessity come to a complete halt.

We should never advance faster than our means permit,

and therefore a national emergency may slow the rate of advance. I assume, however, that the national emergency you are speaking of is the one created by a Communist government, with its spurious claims to social betterment. One way that kind of an emergency can be diminished is to expose these claims to our potential friends abroad by demonstrating the large stake which all persons have in our democratic, free-enterprises way of life.

Q. Have you ever expressed yourself on compulsory health insurance? What is your view?

A. This is a problem about which my information is limited to that of any casual newspaper reader. It seems, unfortunately, to be a controversy which has generated more heat than light. For that reason, I think we have reached a stage requiring more factual inquiry and less expression of opinion. Thas it why I was very much pleased to see the President create an expert commission on our medical needs and why I am encouraged to read that this commission has already begun to hold hearings at which facts are being carefully collected and all points of view heard. I, for one, would be willing to suppress any urge I had to rush into this controversy until after we have had the benefit of the report of this commission.

I am perfectly prepared to say, however, that, whatever the best solution may prove to be, it is clear that the provision of adequate medical treatment for all our citizens is a critically pressing problem. It is so big, indeed, that its solution will probably have to be reached on a tentative and experimental basis, with the observance of some order of priorities which take into account both the needs and our capacities, financial and otherwise, to meet them.

I have, in this regard, been quite impressed by the suggestion that the most pressing problem is the protection of the average family from the illnesses of a catastrophic nature which mean utter financial ruin. If the insurance principle could be brought to bear on these catastrophic illnesses, it would largely eliminate the specter of terror from the average home, but still leave us financially undamaged and professionally independent.

As in most cases, free and easy use of slogans does not seem to me to advance the argument very far in this area. I am against the socialization of the practice of medicine as much as I would be against the socialization of my own profession, the law. Although the provision of adequate legal services to all of our people is by no means a problem of the magnitude of that involved in medical services most lawyers have tried to work toward that goal in the same way that most doctors have done in their field.

I am sure that in both the common objective can largely be realized without the destruction of professional independence, if only we focus on the problems our great good will and good judgment. One thing is as clear as can be, and that is that this matter is much too important to be allowed to bog down in a welter of misunderstanding and partisan politics.

Q. Do you think the Democratic platform should come out in favor of it?

A. In the state of affairs which I have referred to in the answer I have just given you I do not think that the Democratic platform should commit itself to any specific proposal.

I think it should continue its endorsement of the general objective of working toward improvement of the health of our people.

Q. What do you think are going to be the principal issues of the campaign on the domestic side?

A. I think that the domestic issues of the greatest importance to our country and to each of us as individuals are inflation and national solvency. Each housewife in the grocery store is as painfully conscious of prices as the most learned economists and the most experienced financial men. Closely related is federal spending, increasing federal debt and higher taxes. Can these trends be reversed?

A third issue will be widespread disappointment with the revelations of abuse of public trust, and whether it is necessary to turn the national Administration over to another political party in order to deal adequately with this situation.

Q. What do you think are going to be the principal issues of the campaign on the foreign-policy side?

A. There is really only one issue here, and that is whether we continue to counter the threat of Soviet imperialism, by marshaling the resources of the free world. There are, of course, many subsidiary issues growing out of this major one. Few among us, I believe, are really blind to the dangers, and the great debate really revolves around means rather than ends. But means are crucial, and a wrong or impetuous choice can result in disaster. The campaign will be helpful if the foreign policy debate can be carried on honestly and informatively and without exploitation of ignorance and passion.

ADLAI E. STEVENSON

Q. If you had to pick out the biggest single issue of the day, what issue would you choose?

A. Foreign policy, in my opinion. I would view with the utmost misgiving any indication that America was wobbling or indecisive. The continuity of our general post-war policy of resistance to Soviet pressure is the best and only hope of national security and peace.

Inflation and the difficult price, wage and other economic problems which confronts us are all a consequence of our huge effort to redress the balance of power in the world and meet the biggest issue which any individual or any nation can face, the loss of freedom.

Q. How do you think the corruption issue can be answered from the Democratic side?

A. I think the corruption issue has already been largely answered from the Democratic side. The most shocking revelations centered around the Bureau of Internal Revenue. Those exposures were largely the work of a congressional committee headed by a Democratic Representative, Cecil King. It was President Truman who responded promptly with the reorganization plan to take the Bureau of Internal Revenue permanently out of politics, and it was the Democrats in Congress who showed the greatest unity in supporting this proposal against bitter opposition.

I should be the last to pretend that the Democrats in 1952 do not have a heavy load to carry on this issue. But the man in the street knows that no one has a monoply of virtue, least of all a political party. We have learned over the years that honesty in public office cannot be measured by party labels. And we learned in 1923 and 1924 that a political

Stevenson and his sons, left to right, Adlai Ewing III, John Fell and Borden, celebrate Christmas, 1950, in Springfield. Adlai is a senior, Borden a freshman, at Harvard. John Fell goes to Milton Academy. The Stevenson boys spend half of their vacations with Mrs. Stevenson who lives in Chicago.

"Artie" (King Arthur), Stevenson's melancholy Dalmatian, often accompanies him on short walk between Springfield Executive Mansion, where Stevenson has offices in basement, to State House (above) where he has another on second floor. Statue at right is of Abraham Lincoln.

From Chicago Daily News. 1952

Stevenson cartoons in April, 1952, stressed theme of Leap Year, which always coincides with presidential elections.

Rugged routine as Governor includes toasting "Dairy Dream Girl" Irene Bittner in buttermilk (upper left); presenting prize to "Fairy Dancer" Sandra Cheryl Stilwell (upper right); riding in tally-ho with Veep and Mrs. Barkley, Senator and Mrs. Scott Lucas and Mrs. Ives (below) at Illinois State Fair of 1950. Stevenson thrives on such activities.

Stevenson, at head of table in Executive Mansion office, holds weekly Thursday morning conference with administrative staff. Staff members, left to right, are Carl McGowan, William McCormick Blair, Lawrence Irvin, J. Edward Day, Richard J. Nelson, William I. Flanagan, Don Hyndman. Stevenson's entourage is patterned on that of New York's Governor Tom Dewey, whose administrative efficiency Stevenson admires. Governor and one or more of aides often lunch at conference table.

Governor accepts birthday wreath in honor of his predecessor, Governor John Peter Altgeld. Altgeld was celebrated as the "Eagle Forgotten" in poem by the late poet Vachel Lindsay whose house is across the street from Executive Mansion.

Stevenson, who wears horn-rimmed glasses for reading, dictates to his secretary, Miss Carol Evans. Paperweights are golden spike souvenirs. Governor prefers to be photographed from his left.

Right, Stevenson keeps late hours in Executive Mansion, of which he is often the sole occupant. *Below,* Second Man Robert Jones brings Stevenson lunch tray to his office desk. Governor is partial to tomato juice, tomato salad, tomato catsup, tomato highballs and just plain tomatoes, along with other rabbit food.

Courtesy Life, © Time, Inc.

United Press Photo

With son John Fell, Stevenson rides tractor at Libertyville farm, now rented to Marshall Field Jr.

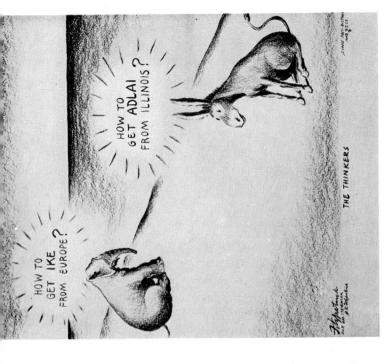

THE THINKERS

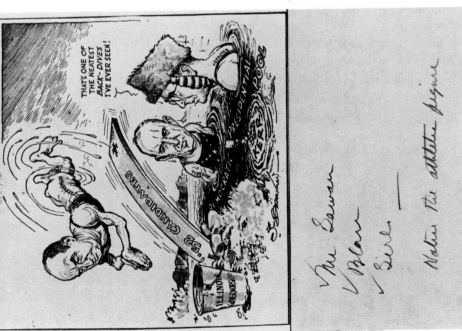

Late April, 1952, cartoons emphasize shocked reaction of politicoes to Stevenson's attempts to decline nomination. Memo under cartoon at left, addressed to office staff, is in Governor's handwriting.

meant when he said, " It is too bad to take my head off. I wanted to see how all this is coming out."

Lets keep our heads, And it isn't always easy, particularly in an election year, and even if you are not running for office! We've come a long way from the myopic era that followed the first world war. One by one these difficulties can be met and mastered — not by star gazing, not by nostalgic yearning for the dear, dead past, not by second guessing "whosiwit" or the painless prescriptions of political medicine men, but by the same practical wisdom and persistence that has served us so well at home in promoting liberty, establishing justice and insuring domestic tranquility.

I am reminded of Robert Frost's Vermont farmer — or maybe he was a Texas rancher. When they told him to hitch his wagon to a star, he said :

I'll hitch my wagon to a horse;
For I've promises to keep
And miles to go before I sleep,

Manuscript of last page of Governor Stevenson's April 22nd speech at Dallas Council on World Affairs contains fewer corrections than usual. The Governor jotted down the lines from Robert Frost from memory.

Stevenson has flown 50,000 miles since his election in 1948—mostly around Illinois in his two-engine Beech-craft.

Stevenson, with former Mayor Edward J. Kelly and Mayor Martin Kennelly (*right*) greets President Truman arriving in Chicago for 1950 Jefferson Jubilee.

Stevenson preserved habitual good humor throughout hue and cry of
1952 presidential boom.

party (in that case the Republican) does not have to get out of office in order to rid itself and the nation of the faithless.

Q. In your experience as Governor, have you found a bipartisan approach on certain issues helpful?

A. Indeed it has. I am proud of the fact that the 1951 session of the Legislature in Illinois enacted a very large number of the proposals contained in my program — and both houses of the Legislature were Republican by comfortable margins. That was possible only thanks to the help and cooperation of a substantial number of Republicans.

It is true, of course, that most of the issues which concern a State government like Illinois bear little relation to the issues which divide us nationally, and I have preached this up and down the length and breadth of our state. But it is quite easy to mix partisan politics into state affairs, the result being too often complete frustration and paralysis. I am genuinely grateful that we have been able to avoid this in Illinois because many members of both parties have exhibited real statesmanship in using the bipartisan approach.

Q. Do you believe in delegating to department heads complete authority, or do you believe in working out the policies in group consultation and then delegating full atuhority to each department head?

A. No chief executive either can, or should, shift responsibility for major-policy formulation to his deparment heads. That is unfair to the latter, and certain to be disastrous to the former, because he will find inevitably that policy has gotten away from his control. I think, therefore, that the top executive should always keep in close touch with the policies of his department heads. Anybody who is good enough to head a deparment should, of course, be trusted in large measure with the execution of policies once evolved in consultation; but, even here, a governor of a state should not, any more than the president of a large corporation, isolate himself completely from familiarity with what is going on in actual administration.

Q. Since you won the 1948 election for Governor by 572,000 and Mr. Truman won by only 34,000, to what do you attribute the success of your campaign — did a large number of Republicans vote for you?

A. The application of a little arithmetic suggests that the answer is "Yes." Illinois has an ancient, however unfortunate and misguided, propensity for voting Republican in state contests, which I can best illustrate by noting that I am the fourth Democratic Governor of Illinois since the Civil War. I think there is no question but that I was the beneficiary in 1948 of a large protest vote which included many numbers of the same political faith as my opponent. I hope those same people will vote for me next November for more positive reasons.

Stevenson's answers to the questions put by U. S. News & World Report were prepared in his office after careful consideration and consultation with his staff. On March 30th, the Governor found himself called upon to give extemporaneous answers to considered questions put to him by four topnotch reporters on the television program "Meet the Press."* The program was telecast the day after President Truman's announcement that he would not be a candidate for reelection. It opened with the announcer's introduction of
*By permission of "Meet the Press" and co-producers Martha Rountree and Lawrence Spivak.

Stevenson and of co-producer Lawrence Spivak and continued as follows:

SPIVAK: Good afternoon, ladies and gentlemen, and welcome to Meet the Press. You've met our guest, distinguished Governor of Illinois, Adlai Stevenson. Now meet our press panel: Mr. Edwin Leahy of the Chicago Daily News, Miss May Craig of the Portland, Main, Press-Herald, Roscoe Drummond of the Christian Science Monitor, and Mr. Richard Wilson of the Des Moines Register and Minneapolis Tribune. And now, Governor, if you're ready, we'll let Miss Craig have the first question.

CRAIG: Governor, last night at the Jefferson-Jackson dinner, all the Democratic leaders were saying why they ought to be re-elected for another four years. Don't you think it's dangerous for one party to stay in so long, dangerous for the country?

STEVENSON: It might be dangerous for the country if the, if its result was the destruction of the two party system. I see no evidence of that. The Republican party looks just as healthy to me as it ever did and a little healthier than it did in the early '30's.

CRAIG: Don't you think the revelations of corruptions reveal you've been in too long?

STEVENSON: Well, I — you saw revelations of corruption in the first years of the Harding administration after it had been in office three years. Do you think that indicated that the Republicans had been in too long?

CRAIG: Well, sir, I was just asking your opinion. Let me ask you this: How do you think the Democrats can clean up themselves? How can that be done?

STEVENSON: I don't see that there's any magic about how you do it. If you find corruption anywhere, you obliterate it. Corruption is treason to a political party, in my opinion, because corruption is disloyal, because it can only breed ill-will for the party. The party itself should be more concerned with destroying corruption within its ranks than even the people themselves.

CRAIG: Well, sir, do you contend that the Democratic party has been diligent in rooting out corruption up to now?

STEVENSON: I'm not contending anything. I was trying to answer your question.

CRAIG: Well, I'm asking you, sir.

STEVENSON: You're asking me do I think it's been diligent? I think once . . .

CRAIG: Yes.

STEVENSON: . . . that these evidences of corruption in the Federal government were brought to the President's attention he has acted. I think his plan to reorganize the Bureau of Internal Revenue was perhaps a wise one. I don't purport to know whether it was wise or not. At least, he made a conscientious effort to take it out of the political arena and put it under the civil service. And I was astonished to observe, if I might say so, that I think some five out of six Republicans in the Senate committee voted against that bill.

SPIVAK: Mr. Leahy?

LEAHY: Governor, President Truman didn't announce his decision to step out until it appeared that Senator Taft's campaign was coming unraveled, and your own reluctance to be a candidate grows by the hour. Would there by any

OF ILLINOIS

chance be any plan to throw this whole ball game to
Eisenhower?

STEVENSON: Well, if there's any such plan, I'm not a part
of it.

SPIVAK: Mr. Wilson?

WILSON: Governor, the atmosphere around here has been
pretty heavily charged with politics, but I want to ask
you a little about Illinois . . .

STEVENSON: That's no secret to me. I've discovered it in the
last 24 hours.

WILSON: Yes, I'm sure you have. I want to ask you a little
about Illinois and the general section of the country.
What do you think the attitude of the people is today?
What do they want? What are they dissatisfied with?
What do they want different?

STEVENSON: I think the — Mrs. Craig suggested one thing.
I think they're very much concerned about the level of
morals in public life. I think naturally they are concerned
about the level of taxes. I think the long and frustrating
ordeal in Korea has been a source of both bewilderment,
confusion, anxiety.

WILSON: Then do you think that the people want to stop
the war in Korea? Do they want lower taxes? How do you
follow that out?

STEVENSON: I think people always want lower taxes, but I
think perhaps, well informed as to the alternatives, they
wouldn't insist on lower taxes at the sacrifice of national
security.

SPIVAK: Mr. Drummond?

STEVENSON: I think there's a general unrest in the country,

Mr. Wilson. That's what I was attempting to say.

WILSON: Well, do you feel that taxes are too high now for the level of national defense? Are the expenditures too high for our own safety and security?

STEVENSON: Seems to me they're certainly too high for our prolonged economic stability, but whether they're too high for our security I don't know. That would be a question that I wouldn't purport to answer.

WILSON: Well, as a man in public life what would you do to meet this situation?

STEVENSON: Well, which situation do you mean, Mr. . . .

WILSON: All three that you referred to, morals, taxes and war.

STEVENSON: I think that government — the moral aspect of your question — is very much like a pump, that you will pump into the government precisely what you pump out of the people, in a government by the people; that the level of morals in public life can never be much different from the level of morals in civilian life.

I think, therefore, that our problem about improving the difficulties in which we're, we have been — we seem to be encountering after, in this anxious age, after two devastating wars. I think government, however, must be, must take the lead and that we must establish precedents and practices in government which, perhaps, we wouldn't even find among our citizenry. It must be like Caesar's wife, unimpeachable.

As to the second aspect of your question, taxes, the tax burden in this country depends — is due largely to the national defense effort. I would say that perhaps it's wiser to spend money which, even in what appears to be excessive quantities, to buy insurance than it would be to risk war and the cost of rebuilding the house. As to the third aspect of your question, if you'll remind me what it is . . .

WILSON: Corruption.

STEVENSON: I've already covered that.

SPIVAK: Corruption, taxes and . . .

VOICES: War.

SPIVAK: . . . war.

WILSON: War.

STEVENSON: I personally am a believer in the so-called post-war policy that's been directed by the Administration of — perhaps I could reduce it to the simple words of assistance and resistance: resistance to the extension of Communist dominion in the world and assistance to the free world to help in that resistance.

SPIVAK: Governor, what do you think would have happened if the United States and the United Nations had not gone into Korea in 1950, June, 1950?

STEVENSON: Well, I think it's very likely — of course, I can't be any more sure of it than you are — I think it's very likely that it would have disillusioned a great many people in the Orient and perhaps in Western Europe. It seems to me had we not met this first armed challenge, this first challenge of the principle of collective security to which we have dedicated both our national policy and so much of our abstance in the post-war era, that it could only have resulted in a sense of alarm, a sense of apprehension and insecurity in the rest of the world with the probability that appeasement by those countries would have followed very rapidly and we would have found ourselves ultimately, if not alone, more or lesse alone.

SPIVAK: Well, Governor, how much of the responsibility for the events that led up to Korea is on the shoulders of those who lead us, and that is the Democratic party?

STEVENSON: The events that led up to Korea?

SPIVAK: Yes.

STEVENSON: Well, I don't know by — what you mean by the events that led up to Korea. If you mean that there is Communism in the world, which is . . .

SPIVAK: No, I meant, I mean what happened in China, for example. I mean what happened about Formosa, for example. I mean the withdrawals of troops from Korea.

STEVENSON: Well, that was pursuant to a resolution adopted by the United Nations, that both the United States and the Soviet Union would withdraw its forces from the Korean peninsula. I think we complied with it in good faith. Whether the Soviet Union did or not I've never been sure. It's possible that we have made errors in Korea. I wouldn't, I'd be the last to dispute it. I would say, however, that the question remains, could we have done anything else than we did in, at the, on the 25th of June, 1950? My own opinion is that we did the only thing that we dared to do at that time.

DRUMMOND: Governor, you have mentioned that you were a supporter of the government policy of assistance and resistance, and I assume that you would agree that the principal measures that have carried out that policy include the Greek-Turkish loan, the Marshall Plan, the North Atlantic Treaty, Mutual Assistance, and so forth. Now since those measures have largely been supported by both parties, do you consider that foreign policy is an issue in this election or that it is seriously at stake?

STEVENSON: Well, Mr. Drummond, I think that foreign policy should be bi-partisan, that our controversy should end, to the extent that that's possible, at the water's edge. I think they are the basic issues in this election. (SIC) Now I don't know what the point of view of the Republican Party will be. I think I know what the point of view of the Democratic Party will be, and I would hope that this election, if it proved nothing else, would serve to remove some of the confusion and some of the misunderstanding that exists on the part of the American people about our, both our responsibilities and where our best self-interest lies in the international field.

CRAIG: Governor, you said once that peace is the unfinished task of our generation. Korea, of course, is the hot spot. What would you do about Korea? What would you do?

STEVENSON: Well, Mrs. Craig, I would personally exhaust every conceivable avenue to bring about a settlement of the hostilities in Korea. I think that what we are doing is about all we can do, and that's to exert every possible effort to settle the Korean incident without enlarging the scope of the war.

CRAIG: It's been since last July now since we've even tried to get a truce. Would you just go on talking at Panmunjom?

STEVENSON: I have no alternatives. I wish I did.

LEAHY: Well, to what avail is all this talk if you insist on shunning a role in national politics, Governor? You have said you don't want a place on the ticket, haven't you, and that you're not seeking it?

STEVENSON: Yes, I've said that I was a candidate for Governor of Illinois, and that's all. That's my aim.

LEAHY: Well, wouldn't your grandfather, Vice-President Stevenson, twirl in his grave if he saw you running away from a chance to be the Democratic nominee in 1952?

STEVENSON: Well, I think we'll have to leave grandfather lie.

SPIVAK: Governor, President Truman said yesterday that he will not be a candidate for the Democratic nomination nor will he accept a draft. Does that describe your position, sir?

STEVENSON: My position, Mr. Spivak — and perhaps I should take this opportunity to try to make it clear if it's not — is that I am an announced candidate for Governor of Illinois. We haven't even had our Illinois primary. I have no other ambitions than to be Governor of Illinois. I do not seek, I will not seek, the Democratic nomination for the Presidency. A man cannot run for two offices at the same time. I've invested something over three years now of hard work, blood and sweat, in the, my job in Illinois. It's been very satisfying and a very rewarding experience for me. I have induced a great many people to come into the state government of Illinois.

What we've been able to accomplish — and I think it's considerable in view of the conditions we found when my administration started— has been largely due to the support and the loyalty of a great many people of all parties in the state of Illinois. I feel a great sense of obligation to a state in which my people have lived for over 120 years.

SPIVAK: Well, Governor, are we to understand from what you have just said that you are requesting that your name not be presented to the convention for the Democratic nomination and that if it is presented that you will ask that it be withdrawn, sir?

STEVENSON: Mr. Spivak, that's a bridge that's more than four months hence, isn't it? It certainly is a bridge that I would not attempt to cross now. I can only tell you what my present state of mind is, and that is that. I'm a candidate for Governor and nothing else, and I seek nothing but that. I hope very much that the people of Illinois will see fit to re-elect me.

WILSON: I merely wanted, Mr. Spivak, to bring out a point there in connection with what the Governor has just said. What is the date of the Illinois primary?

STEVENSON: It's the 8th of April.

WILSON: The 8th of April. Then someone who runs for the Democratic nomination is going to have to get busy pretty soon if you don't run: is that right?

STEVENSON: If I don't run for Governor?

WILSON: Yeah. You haven't got hardly no time at all practically.

STEVENSON: Well, you mean between now and the 8th of April?

WILSON: Yeah.

STEVENSON: Well, practically no time is right, yes.

WILSON: You expect to get the nomination regardless of whether you're nominated for President; is that right?

STEVENSON: Well, I'll be nominated for Governor of Illinois on the Democratic ticket on the 8th of April.

WILSON: Well, then, what's going to happen to the office? Are you just going to vacate it if you're nominated for President?

STEVENSON: You mean after, you mean if I were nominated at the National Convention?

WILSON: Yes.

STEVENSON: Well, if I were nominated and if I accepted the nomination, both of which would seem to me a very remote contingency, that I would accept a nomination that I — hadn't been even offered to me — but granted that that were possible, the law in Illinois is that the State Central Committee selects the successor.

WILSON: Successor. You've considered that possibility already.

(PAUSE)

SPIVAK: You're considering it now, anyhow, aren't you, Governor?

STEVENSON: I've heard about it, I think, for the last 12 or 15 years.

CRAIG: Governor, I've been around here 20 years, and I've heard a lot of ways of talking about things like, "I'm not a candidate" and so forth. General Eisenhower went through that. President Truman said a very simple thing last night. He said, "I shall not accept the nomination." Will you say that, or will you not say that?

STEVENSON: I will not say that. I will say that that's a question that I — a bridge that I can't cross until I come to it, and I see very little likelihood that I'll have to come to it.

CRAIG: Well, then, could I ask you this? Senator Taft told me once that he wanted a lot of things that he thought ought to be done for this country and that the President is the only man that can do them and that's the reason he wants to be President. Now you have the reputation of a crusader in Illinois. You got a lot of things done there. Isn't there any temptation to you to want to do things for this country, too, the whole country?

STEVENSON: Well, I'm glad — you — all down here in Washington have heard about what we've been doing in Illinois.

CRAIG: Oh, yes, we have.

STEVENSON: My temptation is to go on doing, and see if I can finish the job.

CRAIG: But not on a larger scale?

STEVENSON: I don't think the job is ever finished, mind you, and I think we could make permanent some of the things that we have started in these past three years, and I should like to have the opportunity.

CRAIG: But not on a national and international scale?

STEVENSON: I don't see that anybody's panting to have the Governor of Illinois run the country or the, or even the world, for the next few years.

CRAIG: That wasn't an answer, Governor.

STEVENSON: Well, the answer is just what I've said repeatedly, and that is that I am pledged to run for Governor. I must run for Governor. I want to run for Governor. I seek no other office. I have no other ambition.

SPIVAK: Governor, doesn't this large studio audience give you any indication how some of the people of the country feel about that?

STEVENSON: It's very flattering, indeed, and I suppose flattery hurts no one; that is, if he doesn't inhale.

DRUMMOND: Well, I'd like to just remark to the extent of saying that while the Governor seems to be aware of many things, he's not aware of the national interest within his party of his possible nomination, and I think that perhaps in the next few weeks he may become increasingly aware of it and come face to face with a very tough decision he's got to make. But I'd like to suggest that there are a lot of people that would be interested in his views on domestic questions, whether he's a candidate or not, and I wondered if he would indicate a general point of view on such subjects as, say, the Taft-Hartley Law or FEPC . . .

SPIVAK: Well, let's take one question at a time. Are you for or against the Taft-Hartley Law?

STEVENSON: That's like asking me if I'm for or against the tax laws. There are about a, more than a hundred provisions, I think, sections, sub-sections in the Taft-Hartley Law. I couldn't answer it, am I for or against it.

SPIVAK: Would you say generally that it has helped or hurt?

STEVENSON: I think there — I think in some respects it's helped and in other respects it's hurt, and if you were to give me ten minutes I'd try to discuss it. I think the Taft-Hartley Law needs revision, needs substantial amendment. I don't think it should be repealed.

SPIVAK: Now where do you stand on a compulsory FEPC? That's your second question, isn't it, Mr. Drummond?

DRUMMOND: Or on civil rights generally . . .

STEVENSON: You haven't any easy questions, by the way, you'd like to ask me first, have you?

DRUMMOND: All the other easy questions we left outside the room.

STEVENSON: Well, I'd say this: I personally feel that the states regulate as many of the public affairs of this country as they possibly could. I'm a very strong believer that the government concentration of authority in Washington to the extent that that's possible should be arrested. I've written and spoken in that field, as perhaps some of you know, rather extensively. I would hope very much that the problem of civil rights could be administered by the states and administered adequately by the states. To that end, I've tried in the past two sessions of the Illinois legislature to get an FEPC bill passed in Illinois.

If, however, it's impossible to do that, if the states — and I think many of the — one of the reasons why we have such a concentration of authority in Washington is in many cases due to the states' wrongs, failures of states to discharge their responsibilities — if it's impossible for the state to do this job and do it properly, then I would say the Federal government must, because I think ultimately we have to, it's imperative that we move on progressively to give, to realize in practice our professions of faith, and one of our professions of faith is the equality of opportunity of every man, woman, and child in this country, irrespective of race, color, and creed. I think democracy knows no color line.

LEAHY: Governor, I know you have a keen sense of political morality. A question comes up, why can't they solve some of those political assassinations in Cook County?

STEVENSON: That question has arisen in my mind a good many times. I wish I knew the answer.

CRAIG: Governor, there is, amid the general admiration for you, I may say, there is one criticism I hear a good deal, and that is that in the Alger Hiss trial you gave a deposition as a character witness. Would you tell us how that happened?

STEVENSON: Yes. The court in New York before which he was being tried — that was in the first trial, this was in the spring of 1949, as I recall — pursuant to an order of that court, some questions were, interrogatories, as they're called, were sent out to me in Springfield and presented to me by the United States Commissioner for the Springfield district, and the question, in effect, was from what you heard from others, that is, from what others told you, what was Mr. Hiss's reputation for loyalty, integrity, honesty, at the time you knew him in — well, as of that time, in 1948. My answer was that it was good.

SPIVAK: That wasn't your opinion. That was the opinion you said others had of him?

STEVENSON: That was the question that was asked me, was, from what you have heard from others, what is his opinion — what was his reputation? And I would say this, if I might, if you'll permit me to speak a word longer. I'm a lawyer. I think that one of the most fundamental responsibilities, not only of every citizen but particularly of lawyers, is to give testimony in a court of law, to give it honestly and willingly, and it will be a very unhappy day for Anglo-Saxon justice when a man, even a man in public life, is too timid to state what he knows and what he has heard about a defendant in a criminal trial for fear that defendant might later be convicted. That would to me be the ultimate timidity.

DRUMMOND: I've just got one question that bears on the immediate point, and that is now that so many of the facts have come out in the Hiss case, what is your judgement of feeling about the verdict of the court?

STEVENSON: I'm a lawyer. I believe explicitly that a jury of one's peers must find the right answer or else we have no, we can have no faith in our judicial system.

WILSON: Governor, on that point, did you know Alger Hiss when you were in the Agricultural Adjustment Administration?

STEVENSON: I met him first when I was in the AAA where I worked for four and a half months in 1933.

LEAHY: Were you aware of what Whittaker Chambers now calls that Communist Cell which originated in that organization?

STEVENSON: No, I was there in '33 and I don't, I knew nothing about it then. I only knew him very slightly. I was mostly in California.

WILSON: You knew nothing about it. However, you are against loyalty investigations as a general principle, are you not?

STEVENSON: I'm for professional . . .

DRUMMOND: The loyalty investigations as a generality?

STEVENSON: No, on the contrary . . .

WILSON: Well, you say here in a veto message, 'the whole notion of loyalty inquisitions is a natural characteristic of a police state and not democracy.' If you condemn them all, I just wondered if you condemned the McCarran investigation?

STEVENSON: What is the McCarran investigation?

WILSON: Well, the McCarran investigation as you must — should know, at least — is an inquiry in the Senate to find out how deep the roots of Communism go.

STEVENSON: Oh, yes, yes. No, I don't condemn that. I do very much condemn the, what shall we say, the danger of very broad accusations, unsubstantiated charges, which not only endanger . . .

WILSON: That's McCarthyism.

STEVENSON: . . . the reputation of an individual but they actually do an injustice to the republic because we must, we can't let hysteria in our anxiety to prevent any injury to the Bill of Rights, destroy the Bill of Rights itself.

WILSON: Well, you would be in favor of a more scientific investigation.

STEVENSON: That's right. I think the question of Communism and treachery must be ruthlessly pursued. I think, I think . . .

SPIVAK: Sorry, Governor, I'm sorry I have to interrupt you. Our time is up. This concludes the latest edition of Meet the Press. Thank you, Governor Stevenson for being with us.

6

GOVERNOR STEVENSON *has a flair for the neat phrase,
the effective metaphor, the shrewd generalization. Here are
a few capsule comments, chosen at random from his speeches,
writings and conversation:*

Bloomington

There has been a lot of flattering talk on the theme of
"home town boy makes good." It ought to be the other way
around — good home town makes boy.

Races

In our time science and technology have made the world
so small and intergroup contacts so numerous and involved,
that otherwise normal human relations have become fraught
with tension. Racial friction has become a major threat to
the peace and security of all mankind.

Politicians

. . . the worst obstacle and most dangerous symptom of
all is the disdain, derision and disrespect for politics and
politicians by people who should know that politics is gov-

ernment, that it is managed by politicians and that government today is the biggest big business of all.

Free Enterprise

I believe emphatically in what is called for want of a
better word "free enterprise." But free enterprise in our
world must result in more than profit for the few. It must
be a source of well being for the many, or it won't be free
very long.

The Spoils System

Nothing has exasperated me more than to be told that I
ought not to consider appointing a particular person to a
particular job solely because he has been active in a political
party. The issue should be not whether the individual has
interested himself in normal and healthy party activities, but
whether he is honest, competent and qualified for the job.

Big Government

Big government, by comparison with previous standards,
is here to stay. Our government is the largest enterprise on
earth. Its greater centralization has been inevitable because
of the growing complexity of domestic problems, and because
of our enlarged responsibilities in world affairs. The problem
now is to keep government from getting so big, so unwieldy,
and so powerful that it will get out of the hands of the
people. Government in our country must always be the
servant of the people, never the master of the people.

Poor Government

Politicians often speak of "giving" the people good government. But one can't really give good government to the people. Good government is not a gift; it is an achievement. It has a price — the price that must be paid in time and energy and mental sweat in order to understand and to inform others of our problems; the price of examining all sides of public issues; the price of subordinating your own immediate interest to the long range welfare of the whole people.

State Government

As Governor of Illinois, I cannot shape any national or international policies. But I can improve the probity, the efficiency and the morality of state government — or break my heart and head in the attempt. I can influence our policies in education, welfare, taxation and all of the hundred and one housekeeping jobs that are within my province.

Partisanship

Government under our system can never be wholly efficient or perfect, but it certainly can be better; indeed it must be better. And as government descends from the national to the local level partisan divisions diminish in importance. There are few issues at the state level which divide us into Republicans and Democrats, but unhappily we still carry over the convictions — more often prejudices — of national thinking into the local arena. I believe that maturity and understanding will diminish these conflicts.

The Churches

The church teaches the dignity of man and devotion to God and country. These are likewise fundamental precepts of government as we understand it. The stamping out of slavery in every form, the preservation of the rights of individual citizens, the protection of the dignity of man, the elimination of intolerance, and the preservation of religious freedom, all these are things to which the churches and free governments are jointly committed.

The States

If we did not have states we would create them rather than centralize all power at one central point where congestion of authority would soon defeat the purposes and possibilities of democratic participation at the grass roots of our human relationships.

The Average Man

I believe that the average man cares less for politics and party labels than positive performance; that the best government is the best politics, and that any political organization that does not realize that is dead, if not buried.

At Gettysburg

Proud of the past, patient with what Washington called "the impostures of pretended patriotism," it is for us, the living, to rekindle the hot, indignant fires of faith in the free man, free in body, free in mind, free in spirit, free to hold any opinion, free to search and find the truth for himself; the old faith that is ever new — that burned so brightly here at Gettysburg long ago.

The World's Choice

The preservation of the free world hangs upon our ability to win the allegiance of those millions and millions of people throughout the world who have not yet made their choice between our democratic system, on the one hand, and the promises which Communism offers, on the other. That choice will be mainly shaped by our own performance. It will turn upon such things as our ability to avoid the disruptions of depression, to guarantee equality of opportunity, to narrow the gulfs separating economic status, to preserve freedom of thought and action, to make democracy accord in practice with its premises and professions of faith.

Price and Privilege

Our experience has, I think, served to emphasize that while social progress in the legislative field is steady and sure it is sometimes slow. It demonstrates anew that progress in public management almost always lags behind progress in technology and science. But our clumsy, slow way is better than the quick, decisive way of the authoritarian dictators. And when we get impatient to put everything to rights and quickly, perhaps it is well to reflect that delay and frustration are a cheap price to pay for the democratic process and the people's privilege of running their own affairs.

The answer to communism is democracy; not less democracy, or just enough, but more. And democracy is color blind.

Remote Events

We in America today cannot control our own fate and our own future. They are shaped inexorably by events too remote to perceive, too complex to comprehend.

Our Destiny

Destiny has given to this generation another long and hard and bloody struggle to save what our forebears have wrought and to forge a structure for peace which will blot out the evil shadow of tyranny creeping across the earth and let us live in a world where no one drags a chain.

Appeasement

We must prove to the world that we will fight for peace if we have to. We want no more Munichs. We know from sad and bloody experience that appeasement begets more appeasement and finally disaster. We know that the *strong* can't avoid being the *responsible* as well. So we have drawn the sword in unprecedented resistance to cynical, brutal, shameless aggression.

The Human Animal

Man is not only an individual. As Seneca observed, he is also a social animal. But he is something more than an animal. He is endowed by his Creator with inalienable rights. He is a moral agent with the power of making choices affecting not only himself, but countless others. It is because we are more than animals that we can blow ourselves off the face of this planet in the next 50 years. It is also because we are more than animals that we can make this world a better place — better both in material things and in the things of spirit — than it has ever been before.

The Teaching Aim

It has fallen to our lot as it did to the ancient Greeks in their time, and to the Romans in theirs, to make a unique contribution to human history. What is that contribution? I would say it was the realization of an idealist's dream of a free society in which hopes and aspirations once reserved for the few are the property of the many. The American system of public education is both the symbol and the means of our great contribution. To show us the way to this concept of democratic society is the aim of the teacher.

Penny-wisdom

After all, democracy is nothing more than an attempt to apply Christian principles to a human society. Our fore-fathers came together in a common faith in one God. They printed it on their money — "In God We Trust."

The Iron Cage

Time will reveal that the intellectual paralysis of the people, which is the indispensable ingredient of totalitarian-ism, is more deadly to the Soviet system than military weapons.

ADLAI E. STEVENSON

Crime and Country Clubs

Organized crime cannot thrive without the active support of many elements of the community, nor without the passive support of many more elements. The respectable business man who falls for the myth that a wide-open town is good for business is just as effective an accomplice of the criminal as is the politician who seeks to win friends by influencing people. The solid citizen who thinks that illegal slot machines are just fine for his country club but bad for the corner saloon does not realize what difficulties he is making for the person he has elected to enforce the laws.

The Law

Law enforcement doesn't exist in a vacuum, and it can't be considered in isolation. The crisis in law enforcement is but one aspect of the crisis of representative government. Good government is indivisible. You can't expect good government in other departments along with dishonest or ineffective law enforcement, and you can't have effective law enforcement without honest, efficient, responsible government all down the line.

On Russia

I learned at first hand many years ago of the utter incompatibility of our systems but I didn't conclude then nor have I subsequently that peaceful co-existence on the same planet with Soviet Russia is impossible. Devising the means of co-existence will not be easy and will prolong the crisis of our time perhaps for years and years to come.

OF ILLINOIS

On Speeches

I sometimes marvel at the extraordinary docility with which Americans submit to speeches.

The Important Trick

It is hard for some people to grow old without becoming cynical, but I would say to young people: listen to the old and the young courteously but be careful who influences you. If you run across those who see no good in the world, who say that everything is going to the dogs and that most people are rascals, don't believe them. But don't reject wisdom from whatever source it may come. Some of your elders have lived a long time, some of them have learned much. The trick is to select the truly wise ones and listen to them.

The Democrat

"What kind of Democrat I am" makes me feel a little like the old lady who said she didn't know what she thought until she heard what she said. I'm not sure what kind of a Democrat I am, but I am sure what kind of a Democrat I am not. I'm not one of those who believes we should have a democratic regime because it is good for the Democratic Party. If the Democratic party is not good for the nation it is not good for me or for Democrats.

Klu Klux Klan

I am astonished by the reports of burning crosses in the Alton area. They must be the work of individuals and not of organized groups. Illinois will not tolerate the Klu Klux Klan or any organized racial hatred and intimidation.

Freedoms

I don't like doles. I don't like subsidies. I don't like any interferences with free markets, free men and free enterprise. I like freedom to succeed or to fail. But I also know that there can be no real freedom without economic justice, social justice, equality of opportunity and a fair chance for every individual to make the most of himself. And I know that there is little the man on the assembly line or the plow can do to affect the chain of events which may close his factory or foreclose his mortgage. Discontented, desperate men will sell freedom very cheap.

Our Helpful Enemies

I should not be surprised if some day at least an occasional historian referred to this revolutionary era among other things as the age of rediscovery — an interval in which we rediscovered and reexamined many of our concepts, discarded some, exalted others, and generally overhauled a political and economic system that has developed in the careless, expedient, haphazard fashion that orders most affairs of men. If we do, I think we will have our two dread enemies to thank most — Russia and taxes.

Secret Weapon

Self-criticism is democracy's secret weapon. It enables us to periodically re-examine our successes and our failures, our advances and our retreats, on the road toward the fuller expression, and the maximum employment of all our human resources.

Unfinished Business

. . . peace is the most important unfinished business of our generation.